Solutions FOR FAMILIES

PAULA NOBLE FELLINGHAM

FAMILIES NOW, Inc.

For permissions requests, or additional information, please contact the publisher at:

Families Now, Inc.
P.O. Box 37
Austin, Texas 78767-0037

Printed in the United States

10 9 8 7 6 5 4 3 2

ISBN 0-9705497-0-9

TO THE READER

For many years we've been defining the problems families face. Researchers have been busy listing causes for conflicts within the home. How about solutions?

Solutions for Families offers ways to strengthen family relationships. It begins with a Family Survey designed to help family members understand one another's honest feelings. Twenty-four lessons are then presented in a manner that every family can use. In each lesson the concept, activity, discussion and assignment are explained in easy-to-understand terms. All lessons relate to the statements in the Family Survey and include additional activities for family enjoyment.

When the material in *Solutions for Families* is used in homes where there is a desire for improvement, wonderful changes will occur. Families will experience increased love and peace, and relationships will be strengthened in powerful ways.

Strong families can build strong individuals, and those individuals can build the kind of world we all dream of.

The good news is that there are solutions.

It is time for solutions.

ACKNOWLEDGMENTS

Solutions for Families would not have been created in this form without the inspiration and help of Brad Stone and Mark Strong, CEO and president of Families Worldwide. They are men with purity of purpose—to strengthen families around the globe. As a result of their dreams and efforts, thousands of individuals and families have experienced, and will continue to experience, a measure of joy and happiness they never thought possible. I thank them for their kind help, guidance, patience and friendship. As executive director of Families Worldwide, Inc., I appreciate and thoroughly enjoy the opportunity to work with these outstanding individuals.

Solutions for Families is based on the research of three men: Dr. Thomas R. Lee, Utah State University professor and Extension Family Relations Specialist; Dr. Ivan F. Beutler and Dr. Wesley R. Burr, Professors of Family Science at Brigham Young University. The study they completed which had profound relevance for this book, was reported in *Psychological Reports Journal,* Vol. 81, pp. 467-477. These researchers concluded that kindness is the single most important ingredient in a happy home. This concept became the core element in *Solutions for Families.*

A special thanks goes to Benson Schaub Sr., CEO of The American Foundation, based in Scottsdale, Arizona. Benson caught the vision of the Solutions for Families Program and has been extremely supportive of my efforts. I appreciate Mr. Schaub and the outstanding work he is doing to strengthen families.

Marcia Ford, also a champion for the cause of families, has been a tremendous help with this book. Marcia is on the National Board of American Mothers, and her life is an example of the virtues embraced by that fine organization.

A final acknowledgment belongs to my family. My wonderful husband, Gil, has supported and encouraged my desire to help strengthen families. He is an excellent example of one who understands and demonstrates unconditional love. I also give my heartfelt appreciation to the precious young people who inspired many concepts in this book—my seven children: Missy, Angela, Joy, Elise, Danny, David and Benjamin. How richly blessed I am to be their mother. Additionally, I deeply appreciate my sons-in-law, Darin, Darrel and Steve. They have added a new, special dimension of love to our family circle. Our family's search for "solutions" is a never-ending journey, just like yours. I am very grateful to a loving God who gave us families with whom we can share life's adventures.

Paula Noble Fellingham

CONTENTS

INTRODUCTION

Since the beginning of time parents and children have searched for solutions to countless questions and concerns created in the laboratory of the home.

A source of great joy in my life is seeking and discovering solutions for my family—solutions which I can then share with others. Many times during the writing of this book I wanted to sit right down next to you and talk face to face. I am sincerely interested in you and your family. I would delight in your successes, and I would like to help lighten whatever load you carry. With all of my heart I care about strengthening families—yours and mine.

As we begin the adventure of finding solutions, I would like you to feel secure in the knowledge of four things.

First, no matter how unfortunate your past has been—regardless of how many people have failed you in life—you can begin today to make choices which will result in secure, loving relationships.

Second, finding solutions to problems usually requires a willingness to change, learn and unselfishly do "whatever it takes." Change must come from the inside out. No set of rules or suggestions from a book will make a difference unless minds are open and hearts are soft.

Third, because families are groups of individuals, when each family member improves, the whole family becomes stronger. Finding solutions sometimes requires individuals to sacrifice for the good of the whole. Happily, the result of working together to reach common goals often creates "solutions" of improved harmony, unity and love.

Fourth, creating a successful family is a day-by-day (sometimes minute-by-minute) effort. Finding solutions to individual and family problems is a process that takes time and considerable effort. My heartfelt suggestion is to be kind to yourself and patient with your family on your solution-seeking journey. Don't expect immediate success. Remember that there is no perfect family—there are no perfect parents. The key is to learn from mistakes and to keep trying. The rewards of your efforts will be priceless.

How To Use This Book

It is my hope and desire that this book will be a blessing to your family and that you will become familiar and comfortable with it, and use it regularly in your home.

There are four parts to *Solutions for Families:* **Getting Started; Introduction For Parents; Twenty-four Lessons; Solutions Through Stories** and **Poems.**

It is vitally important that you begin by reading the **Getting Started** section. To omit this part of the book would be like trying to build a home without a foundation. There are four important parts of Getting Started: the Family Survey; the Family Contract; the Family Meeting; the Family Goals Statement. Take your time with these exercises. They can be powerful tools to help you build relationships and strengthen your family.

An **Introduction For Parents** is found at the beginning of each chapter. It introduces the subject of the chapter, and the four lessons which follow. It is an opportunity for me to speak to parents about the subject, prior to the lessons they will teach the family. Parents can share information from the Introduction For Parents to enhance the lessons, if they so desire.

The **Twenty-four Lessons** in *Solutions for Families* reflect the twenty-four questions in the Family Survey. The lessons all follow the same format: follow-up from the previous lesson; a concept; family survey review; story and discussion; activity and assignment. The lessons are to be given by a family member, and ideally every person in the family should participate. As much as possible, family members should take turns giving parts of the lesson. For example, one person could read the concept, another family member could share the story and lead the discussion about the story, another could help with the activity and assignment exercises. Of course families can use the lessons however they'd like—there is certainly no wrong way to do it. The key is to meet regularly and use the lessons in whatever way is best for your family.

Solutions Through Stories and Poems are found at the end of each chapter. For most people, the story is a highlight in the lesson. Stories and poems are wonderful teaching tools. I thought your family might enjoy some additional stories and poems for those evenings when you have just a little extra time to spend together. Or perhaps you might enjoy reading them instead of a lesson sometimes. Whatever you choose, the stories and poems are intended to be additional resources, designed to strengthen individuals and families.

Finally, I wanted to share with you some thoughts about the research upon which this book is based. The research cited in the acknowledgments is entitled "Kindness and Unkindness in Families." This research, developed by several university professors, declares kindness to be the single most important ingredient in a happy, effective family. They suggest that kindness "is being gentle, caring, charitable, and concerned for the long-term welfare of others." The study goes on to say that "kindness and unkindness are not roles or tasks people have, rather they are ways of being, ways people relate as they go about their various activities, tasks and roles." This tells me that if we are "gentle, caring, charitable, and concerned for the long-term welfare of others" in our thoughts, words and actions, we will contribute to the happiness and effectiveness of our family, and be good examples of kindness for others.

Could it be that something as simple as kindness is the key to individual and family happiness? And yet, is being kind always an easy "way of being"? As we "go about our various activities, tasks and roles in life," is kindness a virtue that pervades our thoughts, permeates our words, and is perceived in our actions? I understand that being kind is certainly not always an easy "way of being." However, the idea that kindness is a foundation piece in a happy home causes me to believe that finding Solutions for Families is a reachable goal. I thought, "I can do kindness. I can learn to show kindness to my family and others." And I am hoping you will feel the same way.

Now, let us begin the journey of finding solutions for the challenges families face. And please remember, during every step of the way, that we need to be kind and patient with ourselves and family members as we embark on the wonderful adventure of strengthening our families.

Paula Noble Fellingham

GETTING STARTED

Four important steps of *Solutions for Families* will get you started. As you read and participate in these steps, your family will have a great start in laying the foundation of mutual understanding, organization and unity.

1. FAMILY SURVEY

- This is the core of the program and can strengthen your family in powerful ways.
- In the survey each family member responds to statements about your family life.
- After you take the survey and discuss the responses, you'll see how family members really view your family.
- The survey will help you better understand one another. It will show your family strengths, and it will also reveal some things you may want to improve.

2. FAMILY CONTRACT

- This is a contract family members sign indicating their willingness to participate in the Solutions for Families program.

3. FAMILY MEETING

- Holding regular family meetings is the best way to be organized as a family.
- Family meetings have three parts: Family Council; Lesson; Activity.
- This is a good time for families to come together and share their feelings, and plan, learn and play.

4. FAMILY GOALS STATEMENT

- A Family Goals Statement is like your family constitution. It's a statement of your family's beliefs and goals.
- The Goals Statement defines your family rules and values.
- With a Family Goals Statement you'll have direction, and you'll feel more like a team working together.

You can begin the Solutions for Families program by reading the Family Survey Instructions, on the following page, then taking the Family Survey.

FAMILY SURVEY INSTRUCTIONS

The Family Survey is designed to help families understand one another's feelings and how each person views the family. When all family members honestly respond to the survey statements and talk about the results with kindness, the survey can be a powerful tool for family growth.

Each one of the twenty-four lessons in *Solutions for Families* relates directly to the statements in the Family Survey. For example, lesson one, "Kind Thoughts," corresponds to statement one in the survey: "Our family thinks kind thoughts about one another." Completing the survey as a family before you begin the lessons will give you a basic understanding of how family members feel about the issues addressed in the survey. This will aid in your preparation of the lessons and serve as a guide for your discussions.

There are two very important things to remember when you complete the survey and discuss the results. First, family members need to respond to the statements with complete honesty. Tell how you really feel. Second, when your family talks about the statements in the survey, make only positive comments. No family members should feel guilty or challenged because of their honest responses.

Each family member needs his or her own copy of the survey. Additional copies of the survey can be found at the back of this book. You may also photocopy the survey found on page 18 or visit the Families Worldwide website at www.fww.org, where you can download copies of the survey onto your PC. To complete the survey, follow these four steps:

1. Respond to each survey statement twice. The way you respond is by putting either 1 (almost never) 3 (sometimes) or 5 (almost always) beside each statement.

First, respond by thinking about the way your family is right now (actual).

Second, respond by thinking about the way you would like it to be (ideal).

2. Beside each statement write your actual and ideal response numbers. Total these numbers. You'll see that the statements address six areas of family life: Kindness, Commitment, Communication, Choices, Well-being and Spirituality.

3. Calculate the results of all family members' responses. On the left, write each family member's name. Write each person's totals in the chart for each of the six areas.

Add all numbers (actual and ideal). Write the average number below the totals. You'll get the average number by dividing your total by the number of people in your family. For example, if the total number is 50, divide by 5 people in your family, and the average number is 10.

4. Graph the results. Using your average actual numbers, put a dot on the graph above each of the six areas. Put the dot on the graph's vertical dotted line. Connect the dots. Now put x's across the graph, using your average ideal numbers. Connect the x's. You have two graphs: the actual way your family is now, and the ideal way you'd like to be.

F A M I L Y   S U R V E Y

Name_____

Step 1: Choose the number below that you think is the most correct for each statement.

On the left, respond to the statement the way you think your family is now (actual).

On the right, respond the way you would like your family to be (ideal).

Almost Never	**Sometimes**	**Almost Always**
1	**3**	**5**

Actual   Ideal

____   1. Our family thinks kind thoughts about one another.   ____

____   2. In our family we express love for each other.   ____

____   3. We use a kind tone of voice when we speak.   ____

____   4. We treat one another the way we like to be treated.   ____

____   5. We enjoy doing things together as a family.   ____

____   6. We set family goals together.   ____

____   7. Our family helps one another without being asked.   ____

____   8. We have family traditions.   ____

____   9. We try to understand one another's feelings.   ____

____   10. We speak kindly to one another and try not to criticize.   ____

____   11. We listen to each other.   ____

____   12. In our family we can say what we feel.   ____

____   13. We take responsibility for our own mistakes.   ____

____   14. We all help make the rules in our family.   ____

____   15. We try to prevent problems before they occur.   ____

____   16. We can talk about things without arguing.   ____

____   17. Our family has good health habits.
             (We eat healthfully, exercise regularly.)   ____

____   18. We enjoy learning in our family.   ____

____   19. Our family enjoys being with other people.   ____

____   20. Our family makes wise financial decisions.   ____

____   21. We rely upon God.   ____

____   22. Our family prays together.   ____

____   23. We worship God as a family.   ____

____   24. We share our feelings about God in our family.   ____

____ **Total**   **Total** ____

Family Survey Results

Name: _____

Step 2	Results of Individual Responses												
Beside each statement number, write your actual and ideal responses.	**Solutions**												
	Kindness			Commitment			Communication			Choices			Well-Being			Spirituality	

	Kindness			Commitment			Communication			Choices			Well-Being			Spirituality	
	Actual	Ideal		Actual	Ideal		Actual	Ideal		Actual	Ideal		Actual	Ideal		Actual	Ideal
Statement # 1			5			9			13			17			21		
Statement # 2			6			10			14			18			22		
Statement # 3			7			11			15			19			23		
Statement # 4			8			12			16			20			24		
Totals																	

Step 3
Write the totals for each person beside his name. Write the totals and averages at the bottom.

Results of all Family Members' Responses

Family Members' Names	Actual	Ideal	Actual	Ideal	Actual	Ideal	Actual	Ideal	Actual	Ideal	Actual	Ideal
Totals												
Averages												

Graph of Results

Step 4

Using your average actual numbers, put a dot on the graph above each area on the Vertical lines.

Using your average ideal numbers put X's on the vertical lines.

Connect all the dots and X's with a line.

20	20	20	20	20	20
15	15	15	15	15	15
10	10	10	10	10	10
5	5	5	5	5	5

| Kindness | Commitment | Communication | Choices | Well-Being | Spirituality |

Family Survey Results
Example

Name: Linda

Step 2	Results of Individual Responses												
Beside each statement number, write your actual and ideal responses.	Solutions												
	Kindness		Commitment		Communication		Choices		Well-Being		Spirituality		
	Actual	Ideal	Actual	Ideal	Actual	Ideal	Actual	Ideal	Actual	Ideal	Actual	Ideal	
Statement # 1	3	5	5	3	5	9	3	5	13	1	5	17	3	5	21	3	5
Statement # 2	3	5	6	1	5	10	3	5	14	3	5	18	3	5	22	3	5
Statement # 3	3	5	7	1	5	11	1	3	15	3	5	19	3	5	23	3	5
Statement # 4	3	5	8	3	3	12	3	5	16	3	5	20	3	5	24	1	5
Totals	12	20		8	18		10	18		10	20		12	20		10	20

Step 3
Write the totals for each person beside his name. Write the totals and averages at the bottom.

Results of all Family Members' Responses

Family Members' Names	Actual	Ideal	Actual	Ideal	Actual	Ideal	Actual	Ideal	Actual	Ideal	Actual	Ideal
Mom	16	20	18	20	16	20	12	20	14	20	14	20
Dad	18	20	16	20	14	20	10	20	12	20	14	20
Linda	12	20	8	18	10	18	10	20	12	20	10	18
Tom	10	20	10	18	12	20	8	20	10	20	10	20
Totals	56	80	52	76	52	78	40	80	48	80	48	78
Averages	14	20	13	19	13	19	10	20	12	20	12	19

Step 4	Graph of Results
Using your average actual numbers, put a dot on the graph above each area on the Vertical lines. **Using your average ideal numbers put X's on the vertical lines.** **Connect all the dots and X's with a line.**	

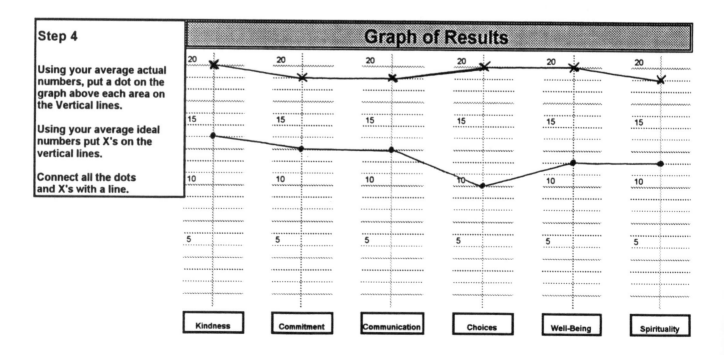

Kindness — Commitment — Communication — Choices — Well-Being — Spirituality

AFTER THE
FAMILY SURVEY

Completing the Family Survey is an important first step in the Solutions for Families program. This survey can become a valuable tool for your family as you discuss your responses to the survey.

Family members need to understand that it is perfectly all right to have different responses. There are no "right" or "wrong" responses. Family members' numbers will often be different because even people in the same family have different beliefs and perceptions. Different is not wrong. It is only different.

Take some time now to discuss your responses. Talk about how the statements made you feel. Remember to make only positive comments during your family discussion.

If you've chosen to complete the graphs, you should have two graphs. One line shows where you are now as a family (actual). The other line shows where you'd like to be (ideal).

As a family, look at your graphs. Based on your results, talk about each of these questions:

1. How do we feel about the kindness we show to one another?
2. How well do we commit our time to each other and to the family?
3. How well do we communicate in our family?
4. How do we feel about the choices we make?
5. How is our family's physical, mental, social and financial well-being?
6. How is our spirituality?

Look at your graphs again. Talk about where you are today and where you want to be.

Decide which areas you want to work on first, then set three family goals. List them on the following page.

FAMILY GOALS

Based on your results from the Family Survey, list the goals your family wants to reach.

GOAL #1 _____

_____

_____

GOAL #2 _____

_____

_____

GOAL #3 _____

_____

_____

FAMILY CONTRACT

The FAMILY CONTRACT is on the following page. When you sign this contract, you are committing your heart and your time to finding solutions that can powerfully strengthen your family. You are pledging your willingness to participate in the *Solutions for Families* lessons and activities.

A concept, activity, discussion and assignment are explained in each of the twenty-four lessons. It is best to approach the lessons with open minds; be willing to learn and grow together. With this positive attitude you'll enjoy finding solutions for your family.

Be confident in the knowledge that the investment of your time strengthening your family will reap long-term rewards of joy in a loving home.

FAMILY CONTRACT

The _____ Family
(Write your name here)

wants to find solutions which will strengthen our family. We commit

to spending time together participating in the

program *Solutions for Families.*

We will meet together and learn the concepts in the lessons. Our

family will participate in the discussions,

activities and assignments.

As we apply these lessons, we can experience greater happiness

and increased love and peace in our home.

Family Members

_____   _____

_____   _____

_____   _____

_____   _____

_____   _____

FAMILY MEETING

Building a successful family is like building a home. Both need a plan. A successful family based on unity and love takes careful planning, but it's worth every moment.

The best way to be organized as a family is to hold weekly family meetings. By doing this, families enjoy a special closeness and stability. Choosing to spend time with your family sends a message more powerful than words. Memories made together during this time will bond and sustain your family through the years.

The family meeting should be an important part of every family's weekly schedule. The family meeting can have three parts. These are suggestions only; your weekly meeting can be anything your family wants it to be.

Parts of the Family Meeting:

- Family Council
- Lesson
- Activity

1. Family Council

The Family Council is a time to do three things: schedule activities, talk about family matters, and plan the next family meeting.

• **Schedule activities.** Coordinating schedules and planning family activities need to be done weekly. When everyone is present (with calendars or note paper), discuss each day of the week. Try to plan a daily schedule that allows your family to eat at least one meal together each day—even if meal time is a little later or earlier than is most convenient for every person. Sometimes individual schedules need to be adjusted for the good of the family.

Talk about upcoming events. Decide when family members can support one another by attending their activities. Then plan one family activity. Remember to talk about all the details of the activity. This will include the date, time, meeting place, money and food needed, special clothes to be worn, etc. When conflicts arise, this family activity has highest priority.

• **Talk about family matters.** Discuss household chores, family problems, and anything a family member wants to talk about.

A family discussion is the core of the family council. This is a valuable opportunity each week to gather around and share feelings about the family. Anything that needs to be discussed can be shared at this time. It is very important that all family members speak only positively, and allow the person talking to share his or her feelings in an atmosphere of empathy and caring. This is a time to voice concerns and suggestions for the good of the family.

• **Plan next week's family meeting.** To make sure that your next family meeting will be a success and each family member will be involved, talk about who will give the lesson, who will help with the activity, and who will prepare the treats.

2. Lesson

The weekly family meeting is an excellent time to teach a lesson. This can be a discussion on correct behavior, good manners, or one of the important moral values which help shape children's characters. The opportunity to meet together regularly as a family to learn "life lessons" is priceless. Parents, this is your stewardship. Unless you teach your children, how will they learn the principles and values you want them to know?

Decide as parents in advance what should be taught each week. A sample lesson on gratitude is included at the end of this section.

3. Activity

The activity is an important part of the family meeting. Families need to have fun together! The activity should be something that everyone enjoys. It could be as simple as a family walk in the neighborhood, or playing a board game. The activity could be watching a movie as a family, going to a sporting event, or doing a service for a friend or neighbor. The most important thing is that the family is all together, enjoying themselves.

As a family, read the following information about a weekly meeting. Then hold a family meeting using as many of the suggestions as possible. Don't be discouraged if your meetings aren't perfect—no family's meetings are. Do your best and congratulate yourselves on participating in an activity that will bring your family closer together.

SUGGESTIONS FOR THE FAMILY MEETING

1. Choose a special time each week that you set aside just for the family.

2. Cut out all distractions during that time—no TV, no homework, no phone.

3. Let family members know that this is the family's time for each other.

4. **Allow family members to take turns being responsible for parts of the meeting.** Family members will feel more involved and will learn more if they participate in the meeting. Children can prepare a poem, story, song, part of the lesson, or refreshments or plan the activity. You may want to rotate the responsibilities of the weekly meeting to involve the entire family.

5. **Adapt the lessons and activities to the needs of your family.** Every family has different strengths and weaknesses. Think about lessons your family needs and activities your family will enjoy. Then plan lessons and activities to meet those needs.

6. **Plan fun family activities.** Time together should be enjoyable. Playing games, cooking, or giving service are some suggestions for weekly meeting activities. The possibilities are limited only by your imagination.

7. **Keep the tone of the meeting positive.** This is a time when each family member should feel loved and accepted. Everyone should be able to speak without being criticized. It can be a time for setting family goals and solving family problems. It should always be a time to enjoy each other. It is most important to be positive and patient. The growth of a child and a family is a gradual process—one day, one act of love at a time. Your family can be built on love and unity with the help of a weekly family meeting.

FAMILY MEETING
SAMPLE AGENDA

Welcome _____

Song/Poem _____

Family Council

    1. Discuss and schedule the week's activities.

    2. Discuss family matters: household chores, family problems, and anything a family member wants to talk about with the family.

    3. Plan next week's family meeting.

Lesson _____

Activity _____

Treats _____

SAMPLE
FAMILY MEETING LESSON
GRATITUDE

Today we're going to talk about gratitude. Gratitude is being thankful for who you are and for things you have.

To begin, let's each name some of the things for which we're grateful.

(The person giving the lesson should now call on one family member at a time, and ask them to name two things they're grateful for. Some answers might be, "I'm grateful for our house, for our family, for my eyes to see, for my ears to hear, for our dog, our food, Grandma, my teacher, my friends, etc.)

Dale Carnegie once said, "Happiness doesn't depend on outward conditions. It depends on inner conditions. It isn't what we have or who we are, or what we are doing that makes us happy or unhappy. It's what we think about it. For example, two people may be in the same place, doing the same thing, and yet one may be miserable and the other happy. Why? Because of a different mental attitude."

Can we be happier if we're grateful for what we have, instead of thinking about what we don't have? How can we acquire an attitude of gratitude?

When we wake up in the morning, we can choose to think thoughts of gratitude or of ingratitude. If we have an attitude of gratitude, instead of thinking about the unpleasant things we have to do that day, we'll think of ways to be grateful. We'll think thoughts like, "I'm glad I can get out of bed and walk. I'm grateful that I have food for breakfast, and that I can see this beautiful day. I'm glad I have a place to go today where people need me."

Do thoughts like those help people be happy? Would other people enjoy being around us because of our good attitude?

I'd like to share with you a poem about gratitude. It's called "The World Is Mine."

The World Is Mine

Today upon a bus, I saw a lovely maid with golden hair.
I envied her—she seemed so gay—and I wished I were as fair.
When suddenly she rose to leave, I saw her hobble down the aisle.
She had one foot and wore a crutch, but as she passed, a smile.
Oh God, forgive me when I whine.
I have two feet—the world is mine!
And then I stopped to buy some sweets.
The lad who sold them was so kind.
I talked with him—he said to me,
"It's nice to talk with folks like you.
You see," he said, "I'm blind."
Oh God, forgive me when I whine.
I have two eyes—the world is mine!
Then walking down the street,
I saw a child with eyes of blue.
He stood and watched the others play.
It seemed he knew not what to do.
I stopped for a moment, then I said,
"Why don't you join the others, dear?"
He looked ahead without a word,
And then I knew he could not hear.
Oh, God, forgive me when I whine.
I have two ears—the world is mine!
With feet to take me where I'd go,
With eyes to see the sunset's glow,
With ears to hear what I would know,
Oh, God, forgive me when I whine.
I'm blessed indeed! The world is mine!

As a family, let's be more grateful each day for who we are and for all we have. Let's each try to keep an attitude of gratitude. I want you to know that I love and appreciate each one of you, and that I'll do my best to have more gratitude.

FAMILY GOALS STATEMENT

A Family Goals Statement is like a family constitution. It is a statement of your beliefs and your goals as a family. It is the definition of the course you want your family to take. Once you have that sense of direction, you can set your long- and short-term goals. You have the vision and values that direct your lives.

Like all families, your family needs to have a clear understanding of where you are going. When you follow a plan, each day will be in harmony with the vision you have of your lives. The steps you take will be in the right direction—toward your personal and family goals.

Define your goals. As a family, decide together what you really want to accomplish. If you don't define your goals, you can get caught up in the "busyness" of life and forget the things that really matter most to you. A great way to start is to create a Family Goals Statement.

Activity

Create a Family Goals Statement. It is important that all family members participate. Everyone should think of things they would like to include.

Example of Family Goal Statement:

The _____Family goal is to have each family member be happy. We will do this by being kind, obeying family rules, supporting one another and serving one another.

In all of our thoughts, words, and actions, we will try to be kind.

We will obey our family rules.

Our rules are: _____

_____

_____

Our family will support each other in our interests and talents by attending one another's activities. We will give service to one another and our neighbors. And we will always love each other.

Someone in your family might say, "Let's be cheerful," or "Let's treat each other the way we want to be treated." Anything the family agrees is a good goal or belief can be added.

Once everyone agrees on the behaviors that are important to your family, write them down. It is your Goals Statement. Put it up somewhere in your home where it can be easily seen.

Discussion

Discuss how a Family Goals Statement can bring greater family happiness. Some answers might be, "Having a Goals Statement in our home will help us act better. Our goals will be on the wall where we can read them often." Or, "With a Family Goals Statement, we'll feel more like a team working together toward family happiness."

Assignment

Read your Family Goals Statement regularly. An ideal time to do this is at the beginning of your weekly family meeting, but any time is fine. Talk about how closely your actions match the goals you decided on as a family. Highlight areas of improvement and discuss as a family what is hindering progress.

Kindness

SOLUTION

INTRODUCTION FOR PARENTS

Kindness is the single most important ingredient in a happy home. This is the conclusion of a family study completed by researchers Dr. Ivan F. Beutler, Dr. Thomas R. Lee and Dr. Wesley R. Burr. Kindness has been chosen as the first and most important "family solution" because it is a key to individual happiness and family peace. Dr. Albert Schweitzer, a well-known humanitarian, once said, "Kindness can accomplish much. As the sun makes ice melt, kindness causes misunderstanding, mistrust and hostility to evaporate."

As I have met with hundreds of families, spoken to numerous groups about family issues, and critically observed families for decades, I have come to know that kindness is indeed a foundational part of every happy home. Without kindness, the money and the time we give our families is meaningless. Where there is no kindness, all attempts at family solidarity are useless.

Kindness can be shown in many ways, every day. We have countless opportunities to show kindness in the home. I've heard it said in different ways but the message is always the same: little, frequent acts of kindness are appreciated far more than large material gifts given without affection. Simple words and deeds that show caring and concern for one another should be a part of the fabric of family life. When we treat one another as we would like to be treated, showing kindness and love, our acts of goodness will be noticed and imitated, creating habits of kindness and traditions of family love.

Parents, I would like to speak to you about four ways we can be kind: in our thoughts, words, tone of voice and actions. These are the four topics of the lessons in this chapter.

First, let's talk about our thoughts. Since our thoughts precede and determine our words and actions, it follows that if our thoughts are kind, our words and actions will also be kind. I believe that the first step in being kind is to think kind thoughts about ourselves. Many times I've heard parents say things like, "I'm not a good mother," or "I'm always yelling at my kids." Parenting is difficult, and it challenges the abilities of us all. However, we need to be kind to ourselves as we parent, by thinking things like, "I may not be doing everything right, but I love my children, I'm trying to learn and improve, and I'm making the best decisions I can." Then if hindsight shows that some of our decisions weren't the best, we can think to ourselves, "I made the best decision I could, with the information I had at the time." And get on with our life. We should learn from mistakes; not beat ourselves up with them. Let's be kind in our thoughts about ourselves.

Also, we should think kindly of family members. It is easy to be offended and easy to dwell on our unkind thoughts toward others. Unkind thoughts can damage souls, tarnish attitudes, and weaken self-images. A better way is to refuse to be offended. Choose to be in control of your own thoughts. Instead of negative thinking, you could think something like, "My son (or any relative) doesn't know how much his remark hurt my feelings. I need to talk to him and let him know how I feel." Then, go to your son and speak kindly and calmly. You could say something like, "Son, when you made that unkind remark I don't think you knew how much you hurt my feelings. When you said that, how did you want me to feel?" Then, hopefully, your son will think about his remarks and your feelings, and you can discuss them.

Another way we can choose to be kind is by the way we speak. Every time we open our mouths to speak we have choices. We can choose to talk to our children kindly, passively or unkindly. For example, we can say kindly, "Honey, will you please shut the door?" Or passively we can say, "Shut the door." A third choice may be to unkindly shout, "Shut the door, stupid!" Lesson Ten, on Positive Words, offers suggestions of how to change negative statements into positive ones. For years our family had a gold decoration on our door with a motto which read, "Kindness Spoken Here." I enjoyed using it as an expression of one of our family goals.

As parents learn quickly, example is the best teacher—for good and for bad. From their earliest years our children imitate our words and actions. If we want children to speak kindly, we need to speak gently. Praise, compliments and acknowledgment of their achievements (no matter how small) are music to their ears, and food for their souls. Self-images are fragile, and need to be handled with kindness. We should speak the way we would like to be spoken to.

Let's talk about the tone of voice we use in our homes. Would we speak to our employer, or best friend, the way we speak to our children? As you will read in Lesson Three, "Kind Tone of Voice," many times it isn't what is said, but rather how it's said that makes people happy or unhappy.

Ways to Show Kindness

1. Speak gently, always being positive and lifting others.
2. Help people, with no thought of reward.
3. Overlook others' mistakes; have great patience with imperfections.
4. Forgive easily and quickly.
5. Put the needs and desires of others before your own.
6. Share the good things in your life freely.
7. Be genuinely interested in the welfare of others.
8. Give of yourself—especially your time.
9. Be polite and courteous.
10. Share another's burden.
11. Listen patiently.
12. Set a good example.
13. Resist the urge to talk about others unkindly.
14. Treat others the way you'd like to be treated.
15. Be fair and honest at all times.
16. Try to love people unconditionally.

K I N D N E S S

Our voices carry a great deal of power, and send messages to those around us. If we want our children to receive a message of love, our tone of voice needs to be kind. When discipline is required, voices can be firm and still send the message, "Even though I dislike what you did, I still love you."

The fourth way we can show kindness is through our actions. They can range from very small acts like a smile, a wink, a touch on the arm, to great acts of sacrifice such as donating a body part to someone who needs it to sustain life. For parents, one of the greatest acts of kindness is to give children our time. By doing this we are giving of ourselves in a way that tells children, "My mom (or dad) loves me. See, she wants to be with me—I am important to her!" It is my belief that children are in our homes for such a short time, we should do all we can to create sweet memories.

In addition to showing kindness in the ways listed above, we can sometimes make a special effort to be kind by scheduling acts of kindness individually and as a family. We can set aside a little time on a regular basis—five minutes, fifteen minutes, an hour—whatever we choose, and not let anything interfere. We should treat this time for showing kindness just like any other important scheduled appointment. This time is for doing something thoughtful. For example, we can call someone who would like to hear from us, write a letter, or as a family perform an act of service. Anything we do will be showing love and making the world a better place.

Showing kindness in the home:

- demonstrates the care and concern family members feel for one another
- creates a loving atmosphere
- prevents problems

We're all happiest when we feel loved—when we know people care about our feelings and have concern for our well-being. Family members show their love to one another through kind thoughts, kind words, kind tones of voice and kind actions. Where there is kindness, there is an atmosphere of love, and problems that weaken families are often prevented.

Kindness can be thought of as a circle. The kindness circle can be broken either by failure to show it, or by failure to receive it. It is equally important to both show kindness and be able to receive it. Usually we parents are so concerned about teaching children how to give that we don't help them learn how to receive. Parents need to teach children to be gracious and return kindness with words and expressions of gratitude. For example, thank you notes sent to gift-givers are always appreciated, and often result in desires to give again. Simple smiles and words of appreciation following acts of kindness help keep the "circle of kindness" intact. Russell Lynes said, "The art of acceptance is the art of making someone who has done you a small favor wish that he might have done you a greater one."

You may not believe that your family can generously show kindnesses to one another because perhaps your parents didn't show kindness in your home. This is a challenge. Although you cannot change your past, you do have the power to affect your future; to choose how you think and act. You can choose to begin new traditions of kindness in your home. It will be more difficult than if examples of kindness were part of your heritage, but you can practice kindness in your family and leave a legacy of love for your children and grandchildren.

Kindness is the single most important ingredient in a happy home. Henri Frederic Amiel reminds us of the importance of this great virtue with his words "Life is short and we have never too much time for gladdening the hearts of those who are traveling the dark journey with us. Oh, be swift to love...make haste to be kind."

LESSON ONE

Kind Thoughts

Concept

Kind thoughts are pleasant ideas that lift the soul. They always come before kind words and actions. How we think determines how we act.

If we want to become kinder people, the first step is to recognize that kindness, and unkindness, begin in our own minds. We can choose to think good thoughts, no matter what is happening around us.

If we're aware of our thoughts, we can better control our words and actions. We need to be aware of what we're thinking, and try to catch ourselves in the act of thinking unkind thoughts. When we notice that our thoughts are unkind, we can say to ourselves, "That wasn't kind." Each time we catch ourselves thinking a negative thought, we should try to replace it with a positive one. That way we can prevent unkindness. Once we start paying attention to our thoughts, we'll discover that we can better control what we say and how we act. Then we'll be on the road to becoming the kind people we want to be.

If unkind thoughts about another person do occasionally creep into our minds, we can react kindly by trying to imagine what it would be like to be him, with his life, his needs and desires. We should then think about that person in the same kind way we'd want him to think about us.

We may believe that if others were kinder to us, we could be more kind. Or we might think that our problems in life keep us from being happy and as kind as we should be. Alfred D'Souza once observed, "For a long time it seemed to me that life was about to begin—real life. But there was always some obstacle in the way, something to go through first, some unfinished business, time still to be served, a debt to be paid. Then life would begin. At last it dawned on me that these obstacles were my life." Having kind, positive thoughts toward others, and our circumstances, is a wonderful step toward living a happy, abundant life.

Family Survey Review

Statement # 1. Our family thinks kind thoughts about each other.

- Let's name some kind things we can think about each other.
- What is an example of how we can replace an unkind thought with a kind one?

STORY

Jayne Fisher watched anxiously as her 17-year-old daughter Katie pulled her unruly lamb into the arena of the Madison County Junior Livestock sale. With luck, Katie wouldn't collapse, as she had during a livestock show the day before.

Katie was battling cancer. This was her first chance in months to be outdoors having fun, away from hospitals and chemotherapy treatments, and she had come with high hopes of earning some spending money. She had wavered a little on her decision to part with the lamb, but with lamb averaging two dollars a pound, Katie was looking forward to receiving some much-needed money. So she centered the lamb for viewing, and the bidding began.

That's when Roger Wilson, the auctioneer, had a sudden inspiration that brought some unexpected results. "We sort of let folks know that Katie had a situation that wasn't too pleasant," is how he tells it. He hoped that his introduction would push the bidding up, at least a little bit.

Well, the lamb sold for $11.50 a pound, but things didn't stop there. The buyer paid up, then decided to give the lamb back so that it could be sold again.

That started a chain reaction, with families buying the animal and giving it back, over and over again. When local businesses started buying and returning, the earnings really began to pile up. The first sale is the only one Katie's mom remembers. After that, she was crying too hard as the crowd kept shouting, "Re-sell! Re-sell!"

Katie's lamb was sold 36 times that day, and the last buyer gave it back for good. Katie ended up with more than $16,000 for a fund to pay her medical expenses—and she still got to keep her famous lamb.

Discussion

1. Why did the crowd at the livestock sale think kind thoughts about Katie?

2. How did the thoughts of the crowd determine their actions? (*Their kind thoughts about Katie led to higher bids to help her.*)

3. What can we do when unkind thoughts enter our mind?

Activity

We're each going to take a turn and share one kind thought about every family member. (*One person might say, "Mom is a good cook." The second person might say, "Dad listens to my problems."*) One by one, every person in our family will have a turn listening to one kind thought about themselves from each family member.

Assignment

1. During the coming week, make a real effort to have kind thoughts. If you should catch yourself with an unkind thought, recognize it and replace it with a pleasant thought.

2. Choose one person in the family, and try to be very sensitive to his or her feelings for one week. Make a special effort to really feel what that person is feeling, and think about him in the same way you'd like him to think about you.

3. Participate as a family in the activity that follows this lesson: Family Time Capsule.

ACTIVITY

FAMILY TIME CAPSULE

Most people have strong feelings about what it means to be a member of their family. This activity is an opportunity for family members to share those feelings of why their family is important to them.

Activity

1. Give each family member an envelope to hold any of the following:

   - Favorite keepsakes acquired during the past year (awards, letters, etc.)
   - Newspaper clippings, school report cards, original poems, etc.
   - Anything else that represents the person's hobbies or interests.
   - Photos of themselves, friends, activities.

2. Give everyone an index card or paper to write down his or her name, the date, plus any or all the following:

   - Names of friends.
   - Something they enjoyed this year.
   - Something they want to remember about the year.
   - Something they're proud of.
   - A goal they have for the next year.
   - Advice they'd like to give themselves for the next year.

3. Put the card in the envelope.

4. After everyone has filled their envelopes, on another piece of paper suggest they write a short note to each family member for that person to put in his envelope. Notes could include compliments, a special memory, or a wish you have for that person.

5. When all of the envelopes have been filled, seal them, put them in the box along with anything else your family would like, and seal it.

6. Write the date—in exactly one year—when you will open the box. In one year, open the family box and enjoy your memories.

L E S S O N   T W O

Kind Words

Follow-up

(As a family, discuss the assignment for the lesson Kind Thoughts.)

1. How are we each doing with recognizing our unkind thoughts and trying to make them more pleasant?
2. Does someone have an experience they would like to share about thinking of others kindly?

Concept

The sainted Catholic nun Mother Teresa said, "Kind words can be short and easy to speak, but their echoes are truly endless." Kind words have the power to heal and to lift. Speaking kindly shows that we care about the person we're talking to. We all feel good when we say kind things to others and when kind things are said to us. On the other hand, when we're spoken to harshly, it is easy to lash back defensively and speak unkindly. Along with harsh words come unpleasant feelings, such as anger, sadness, and regret.

When we speak negatively it focuses our attention on what is wrong with our world and our circumstances. It doesn't help improve things, it makes our life worse.

An unkind remark to another person can range from seemingly harmless to truly hurtful. The truth is, however, whether we're being simply sarcastic or intently cruel, the effects are similar. Both types of remarks leave the giver and the receiver feeling negative and critical. The reverse is also true. When we speak kindly of others it focuses our attention on their goodness. When we speak kindly of our circumstances it turns our thoughts toward gratitude for what we have.

Here's an example of how one person chose to speak kindly to a stranger:

A gentleman in the grocery store waited at the check-out while a young mother struggled with two children. As the man watched the scene he noticed how incredibly patient the check-out clerk was.

The clerk calmed the young mother, helped her with her coupons, and even held the baby while the woman counted her money.

After the mother left, the gentleman said to the clerk, "I'm so impressed with your patience and kindness with that customer."

The clerk looked at him sincerely and said, "Thank you, sir. You are the first customer in eight years to give me a compliment."

We will be delighted to discover that as we notice and acknowledge people's goodness, that is what we will see. We will recognize the beautiful rose instead of the thorn, the glass half full instead of half empty. We will enjoy a dimension of love and gratitude which will spread contagiously to others and help us be a force for good in the world.

Family Survey Review

Statement # 2. We express love for each other.

- How do we express love for each other in our family?
- What are some of the words we say that show we love each other?

STORY

It was an unseasonably hot day. Everybody, it seemed, was looking for some kind of relief, so an ice cream store was a natural place to stop.

A little girl, clutching her money tightly, entered the store. Before she could say a word, the store clerk sharply told her to get outside and read the sign on the door, and to stay out until she put on some shoes. She left slowly, and a big man followed her out of the store.

He watched as she stood in front of the store and read the sign: No Bare Feet. Tears started rolling down her cheeks as she turned and walked away. Just then the big man called to her. Sitting down on the curb, he took off his size 12 shoes, and set them in front of the girl saying, "Here, you won't be able to walk in these, but if you sort of slide along, you can get your ice cream cone."

Then he lifted the little girl up and set her feet into the shoes. "Take your time," he said. "I get tired of moving them around, and it will feel good to just sit here and eat my ice cream." The shining eyes of the little girl could not be missed as she shuffled up to the counter and ordered her ice cream cone.

He was a big man, all right. Big body, big shoes, but most of all, he had a big heart.

Discussion

1. Why do you think the man in the story gave his shoes to the little girl?
2. Do we sometimes think kind thoughts, but we're too afraid to say them? What are we afraid of?

Activity

For our activity we're going to read The Power of Appreciation on the following page, and do one (or more, if you'd like) of the activities included there.

Assignment

Choose one or more of the following assignments:

1. With everyone participating, name five kind things you can say to make someone happy.
2. Make a special effort to use kind words in your home.
3. All family members give one compliment each day for a week.

THE POWER OF APPRECIATION

One of the important ways to communicate love in families is to express appreciation. We all enjoy being with people who make us feel good about ourselves. Family members who make the effort to notice the good things we do and express their thoughts of appreciation help us feel good. When we feel good about ourselves it's easier to give to others.

Think of an experience you've had trying to do something nice for someone, only to have it go unappreciated. Have you ever expected to hear praise and instead you were criticized? Let's compare this with an athletic game. Imagine yourself trying to learn a new game. You've been told the rules by an official, and you are now on the field ready to play. The game begins and you start playing the way you think you're supposed to, when suddenly the official blows the whistle and calls you over. The official explains what you did wrong, which is different from what you remember being told before the game. He gives you a warning to play by the rules. The action begins again but is stopped almost immediately, and the official scolds you again. Imagine this is repeated each time the game is started. No matter what you do, it's wrong.

You would quickly begin to feel confused and frustrated. Depending on your personality, you might become withdrawn and discouraged, or you might become angry and aggressive at constantly being stopped. You might decide the game isn't worth playing.

Unfortunately, all too often families get into a pattern like this. People are trying their best, but the focus is on what they do wrong rather than on what they do right. We often think that in order for someone to learn or improve, we need to criticize what they did wrong.

Answer three questions:

1. Do we like it when people criticize us?
2. Do we want to share our thoughts and concerns with them?
3. How do we feel about ourselves when we're criticized?

Criticizing others not only creates bad feelings, it isn't a good way to get people to change. It's a fact that animals can be trained much faster if they're rewarded for each correct attempt rather than being punished each time they fail. This principle holds true for people, too. We improve our performance faster with praise than with criticism.

It seems to be a law of human behavior that how we act is contagious. In other words, if we are kind to others in our family, we receive kindness in return. It's also true that our usual response when someone criticizes us is to criticize them in return. In families, it is especially important that we avoid the vicious cycle of criticism which always hurts relationships.

William James, considered by many to be the greatest American psychologist, wrote a book on human needs. Years after the book was published he remarked that he had forgotten to include the most important need of all—the need to be appreciated. Establish an atmosphere of appreciation in your family by overlooking the negative and "catching" one another doing good things.

Expressing appreciation is not difficult. It requires making the effort to notice the positive things that happen, and telling the person involved how you feel about it. If Mom doesn't get a sale she has been working on, other family members can remind her that she got three last week. If a child doesn't do well in one subject, parents can point out his good grades in other areas.

Three Appreciation Activities

Activity 1. Showing Appreciation

Have each family member put his name at the top of a piece of paper. Each one should then pass his paper to the person on his right. The recipient then writes something specific the giver has done which they appreciate. On the bottom of the page the writer then folds the paper over to conceal what's written, and passes it to the next person. After everyone has his paper back, he can read what others have written. Then taking turns, have everyone say something about your family that he appreciates. Be specific about some behavior rather than the more general "We're nice to each other." An example of a specific behavior may be: "I like it when we go on walks together."

Activity 2. Expressing Affection

Family members, including husbands and wives, often think it is not necessary to say, "You are wonderful!" to each other. Everyone needs to know they are needed, appreciated, respected and admired. Telling your spouse or other family members why they are important to you is a good way to keep your relationships healthy. The following activity can help you share some of your feelings:

1. Make a list of reasons why you love your spouse or other family members.
2. On each day of a calendar (for a week or a month) write one reason why you appreciate them.
3. Decorate the gift calendar with stickers, pictures, clippings, etc.

4. Give the calendar to your spouse or family member as a way to express your feelings for them.

Activity 3. Noticing Good Qualities

In strong families people truly care about one another's well-being, and they say so. The following activity can help family members notice the good things about each other.

1. Suggest that family members make a real effort to look for things they like about each other. These might be:

• Talents, skills, and achievements
• Qualities and characteristics that make the person special
• Something nice the person did or said

2. Encourage family members to let each other know how they feel by writing short notes about the things they have noticed.

Example: Mom, you made a super dinner! Love, Judy

3. Put the notes under the person's pillow, or in a backpack, lunch bag, desk, etc.

4. Write at least one note to each family member every month.

Kind Tone of Voice

Follow-up

(As a family discuss the assignment for the lesson Kind Words.)

1. How are we doing with using kind words in our family?
2. Who can tell us about a compliment they gave, or tell about a compliment received from a family member?

Concept

Many times it isn't what is said, but rather how it's said that makes people happy or unhappy. One way to show kindness is to use a gentle tone of voice when we speak. It takes great effort at times, but speaking kindly can become a habit.

Our voices carry a great deal of power and send messages to those around us. When we speak loudly and harshly, people around us often feel upset. On the other hand, when we speak kindly it encourages feelings of love, calmness and respect.

As we speak with gentle tones, we'll discover improved feelings in our home, and we'll help create a loving atmosphere. Additionally, when our voice is

controlled, we feel better about ourselves than when we lose control. Because we teach best through our example, those who speak with gentle voices will be pleased to hear others speak that way too.

Another benefit is that calm voices lead to good behavior. If we want our family to behave with love towards one another, one of the best things we can do is to speak gently. It makes sense that the opposite is also true. If we want others to behave well, one of the worst things we can do is speak harshly.

Using a kind tone of voice will help us prevent family problems, make our home a nice place to be, and deepen the love we feel for one another.

Family Survey Review

Statement # 3. We use a kind tone of voice when we speak.

- How will speaking kindly in our family make a difference in the atmosphere of our home?
- How can we each improve a little in this area?

STORY

John had a long, difficult day at work. He was exhausted. While he was driving home, John passed a park and noticed a young father playing with his two sons. They were laughing and enjoying themselves. John thought about his own children. He knew he could be a better father.

As John continued on toward home, he made a decision. John decided that no matter what happened that evening, he would use a kind tone of voice. Even though he was tired, John promised himself he'd speak kindly.

When John arrived home his wife asked how his day had been. Instead of his usual grumbling about problems at work, John cheerfully replied, "Well, things could've been better, but I'm sure glad to be home!"

All evening John spoke kindly to his wife and children. Even when an irritated employee phoned and angrily complained about work, John responded calmly and kindly. An amazing thing happened. John set the tone of kindness in the home, and his family followed his example. Just before bedtime, Matthew, one of the children, said, "Gosh, something is different around here. Everybody's so—so happy!"

John then told his family about the decision he had made on the way home from work after he saw the young father playing in the park with his sons. John confessed that he had no idea what a difference using a kind tone of voice could make in their home. Matthew spoke up and asked, "Hey, Dad, does that mean we can go play ball in the park tomorrow?" They all laughed, and John agreed to take him.

Discussion

1. What is the first step we need to take to change our behavior? *(Recognize that improvement is needed.)*
2. What happened to help John recognize that he needed to be a better father? *(He saw a man playing with his sons and knew he could improve.)*
3. What was one way John decided he could improve? *(Use a kind tone of voice with his family.)*
4. Is it sometimes easier to speak more pleasantly to our friends than to our family? Why?

Activity

There are five sentences we're going to read out loud together. First we'll say them unkindly, then we'll say the same sentence using a kind tone of voice. *(Hold up the page so everyone can read it together.)*

1. COME TO BREAKFAST.

2. WE'RE GOING TO BE LATE.

3. SHUT THE DOOR.

4. CAN YOU LISTEN TO ME?

5. I WANT YOU TO UNDERSTAND.

Assignment

During the coming week if you use a harsh tone of voice, immediately repeat what you said, using a better tone of voice. You'll be amazed at how soon you can change, until using a kind tone of voice becomes a habit.

For example, parents with young children: If your child yells, "Mama, tie my shoe!" You say, "Tone of voice." Then you use a kind tone of voice and say, "Mama, please tie my shoe." Have the child repeat your example exactly. When he has spoken correctly, you exclaim, "Yes! That's the right way we talk!" and give him a hug.

For parents with older children: Speak kindly—be an example to them. When parents speak calmly, they can often diffuse anger. Further, parents shouldn't allow disrespectful, unkind talk in their homes. It is their responsibility to be good examples in teaching their children to be kind.

LESSON FOUR

Kind Actions

Follow-up

(As a family discuss the assignment for the lesson Tone of Voice.)

1. Can anyone remember a time this week when you felt like using an unkind tone of voice, but spoke gently instead?
2. How can we make speaking kindly a habit?

Concept

Kind actions are anything we do to make a person's life easier or happier without expecting a reward. Kind actions show concern and caring. When we show kindness in our family, we're helping one another feel loved. When people feel loved, they can more easily show kindness to others.

Mother Teresa encouraged everyone to be kind when she said, "Spread love wherever you go: first of all in your own house. Give love to your children, to your wife or husband, to a next door neighbor. ...Let no one ever come to you without leaving better and happier. Be the living expression of God's kindness; kindness in your face, kindness in your eyes, kindness in your smile, kindness in your warm greeting."

Kind actions can be very simple—a smile, a pat on the back, helping with a chore, listening with interest when someone needs you, or doing a job that needs to be done without being told. When family members ask themselves the question, "What can I do to make another person's life easier?" or, "What can I do to help someone I love?" there are usually countless answers. Being in a family gives us many opportunities to show kindness every day.

Our kind actions come from our thoughts—the desires we have to be good and loving. At the end of each day we should think, "How closely did my actions today match my good intentions to be kind?" Being aware of our actions will help us improve them day by day, until we become truly kind in thought, word, and deed.

Family Survey Review

Statement #4. We treat one another the way we like to be treated.

- Is this true in our family?
- What can we do to live the "Golden Rule?" (Do unto others as you would have others do unto you.) Suggestions: We can try to understand the other person's feelings before we speak or act. Also, we can ask ourselves the question, "Would I want them to treat me this way?

STORY

Several years ago at the U.S.A. Special Olympics in Seattle, Washington, nine contestants assembled at the starting line for the 100 yard dash. Every runner was either physically or mentally disabled. At the sound of the gun they all started out, not exactly in a dash, but each with great excitement to run the race to the finish and win.

Suddenly, one boy stumbled on the asphalt and fell. He lay on the ground and cried. When the other contestants heard the boy crying, they slowed down and stopped. Then all eight of those special young people turned around and went back. One girl with Down's syndrome bent down and kissed him, saying, "This will make it better." They picked up their fallen competitor, then all nine linked arms and, grinning broadly, they walked together to the finish line.

Everyone in the stadium that day was touched by the compassionate act of kindness they had witnessed. The entire audience unanimously gave the runners a long, enthusiastic standing ovation.

Discussion

1. Do you think each young person wanted to win?
2. When one boy stumbled, what did the runners do?
3. If you were a runner that day, do you think you would have stopped? Why or why not?

Activity

For our activity, let's each think of a time when someone in our family was kind. The one who begins will explain what kindness was shown. We won't tell yet who the kind person was. Let the family guess. The one who guesses right is the next one to tell about someone being kind. Each time, the person who showed the kindness is to keep quiet. This is an example of how it will work: One person will say, "Someone made a great dinner for the family tonight. Who is it?" Or, "Someone helped me with my homework. Who is it?" If the children are small, Dad may say something like, "Someone ran to the corner to meet me when I got off the bus. Who is it?"

No one gets a second turn until everyone has had one turn. The game can continue as long as everyone wants to play. (*If your family is small, acts of kindness by grandparents and friends can be shared.*)

Assignment

1. Answer these questions:

• If someone in my family is unkind to me, am I unkind to them to get even?
• Do my actions show that I love my family?

2. Do at least one kind thing for each family member during the coming week. Anonymous acts of kindness are even more special.
3. If you wish, read the Additional Solution for Success: Giving and Receiving Affection.

KIND ACTIONS

GIVING AND RECEIVING AFFECTION

Some years ago, hospitals and orphanages discovered a fascinating phenomenon known as the "Failure to Thrive" syndrome. Babies who were in the hospital for a long time began to lose weight, they were not learning to sit up or crawl, and they didn't show any interest in what was going on around them. In some cases, they even died. At first, authorities were very puzzled by the problem. These babies were being cared for physically in every way that was needed. Doctors came to realize that these babies were not receiving enough affection. Nurses were told to hold the babies often, and to take time from their duties to talk and sing to the babies. Miraculously, the babies began to grow and progress. Today, most hospitals have a rocking chair in the nursery for nurses and volunteers to hold and rock babies regularly.

None of us really outgrow our need for affection. The outward signs may not be as clear as with small babies, but many people "fail to thrive" because of lack of affection. We all have a need to receive affection if we are to become the best we can be. We also need to give affection freely so others know we care.

People express affection in different ways. Some are more comfortable than others in giving and receiving affection. For some it is very natural to give kisses, hugs or pats on the back. For others this can seem awkward. Some people find it easy to speak warmly and affectionately. For others, doing something for someone is their way of showing affection. It should also be remembered that children have different personalities and sometimes prefer different expressions of affection.

Family members need to make an effort to show appropriate affection for each other in a sensitive way that allows all family members to feel comfortable. You can determine appropriate ways to show affection to each family member by asking the following questions:

- When you are feeling upset, what can someone do to show they care about you?
- If you had just received an award, how could someone show they are happy for you?
- When you want to show someone you care, would you be more likely to do something special for them, praise them, or give them a hug?

Listen to how everyone answers each question, one question at a time. The different ways people express affection is just one of the many differences between us. Differences aren't wrong or bad, they are just differences. One of the greatest ways to show someone we truly care about them is to accept them the way they are. Acceptance is a great source of support to people. It says, "You don't have to change for me. I like you just the way you are."

The giving and receiving of affection in a family is one of the indications of strength or weakness. Families should give and receive affection freely. The benefits of showing genuine love and kindness to one another will be felt for generations.

KINDNESS

Loving Time

A few years ago when I returned to teaching, I was assigned a first grade class. I was a bit apprehensive, since always before I had taught upper grades.

One of my first actions was to eliminate the "Show-and-Tell" period, since I felt that the children who had something to talk about did not require practice in communication, and that the shy ones who needed to speak out were reluctant to do so.

One of the shy ones in this class was a small, curly-haired girl named Teresa. After my announcement, Teresa came to me with a request:

"Mrs. Silva, instead of 'Show-and-Tell,' can we have a loving time?"

I was not quite sure what she meant, so I asked her to explain. I hope the years will never allow me to forget her answer:

"Every once in a while you could lift us and give us a hug, and we could tell you something important. It wouldn't take long."

So from that day on, whenever a child needed "loving," he would stand close to my desk and receive a hug, a pat, and a few moments of my undivided attention while he told me something "important." We had such a good class that year–it was the year my students taught me.

— Myrtle Silva

What Is Love?

The story of how Anne Sullivan taught deaf, mute, blind Helen Keller to communicate with others is one of tenderness, courage, and devotion. Helen's perception of the word "love" is an example.

Miss Sullivan had spelled into Helen's hand, "I love Helen."

"What is love?" Helen asked, but was unable to understand Miss Sullivan's attempt to explain.

A day or two later it had been cloudy, and then suddenly the sun broke forth in warmth.

"Is this not love?" Helen asked.

"Love is something like the clouds that were in the sky before the sun came out," Miss Sullivan replied. "You cannot touch the clouds, you know; but you feel the rain and know how glad the flowers and the thirsty earth are to have it after a hot day. You cannot touch love either; but you feel the sweetness that it pours into everything. Without love you would not be happy or want to play."

"Truth burst upon my mind," Helen wrote later. "I felt that there were invisible lines stretched between my spirit and the spirit of others."

— Author Unknown

The King's Highway

Once a king had a great highway built for the members of his kingdom. After it was completed, but before it was opened to the public, the king decided to have a contest. He invited as many as desired to participate. Their challenge was to see who could travel the highway best.

On the day of the contest the people came. Some of them had fine chariots, some had fine clothing, fine hairdos, or great food. Some young men came in their track clothes and ran along the highway. People traveled the highway all day, but each one, when he arrived at the end, complained to the king that there was a large pile of rocks and debris left on the road at one spot, and this got in their way and hindered their travel.

At the end of the day, a lone traveler crossed the finish line and wearily walked over to the king. He was tired and dirty, but he addressed the king with great respect and handed him a bag of gold. He explained, "I stopped along the way to clear away a pile of rocks and debris that was blocking the road. This bag of gold was under it all, and I want you to return it to its rightful owner."

The king replied, "You are the rightful owner."

The traveler replied, "Oh no, this is not mine. I've never known such money."

"Oh yes," said the king, "you've earned this gold, for you won my contest. He who travels the road best is he who makes the road smoother for those who will follow."

—Author Unknown

The Puppy

A small boy once inquired about puppies for sale at a home in a well-to-do neighborhood. Noticing that the little one was dressed poorly, the lady of the house replied, "Oh, but they're very expensive—fifteen dollars each."

The boy replied, "I have only two dollars."

"I'm sorry."

"But I heard there was one with a bad leg. May I look at him?"

"Well, certainly, if you wish."

Arriving in the garage, the boy quickly spotted the crippled pup, picked it up and began stealing its heart with his natural affection for it.

"I'd sure like to have this dog, ma'am."

"But surely you don't want a crippled dog."

The little one raised his pant leg to reveal a brace that he had worn since being afflicted with polio, and said, "I think he needs someone who understands him."

The boy returned home that day with a loving pet, and two dollars.

— Author Unknown

You're So Kind

When I first went to work as a nurse in an old folks' home, they gave me the most difficult cases, and one was an old woman who used to sit in a rocking chair all day long. Nobody liked her. The other nurses avoided her, and that's why I was given the assignment. I thought to myself, "If the Christian message of love means anything, it means something now with this woman." So I pulled up a rocking chair and just rocked alongside this woman and loved her and loved her. The third day she opened her eyes and said, "You're so kind." Those were the first words she had spoken in three years. Two weeks later she was out of the home.

— *Guideposts* magazine

The Value of A Smile

It costs nothing, but creates much.

It enriches those who receive, without impoverishing those who give.

It happens in a flash, and the memory of it sometimes lasts forever.

None are so rich that they can get along without it, and none are so poor but are richer for its benefits.

It creates happiness in the home, fosters good will in a business, and is the countersign of friends.

It is rest to the weary, daylight to the discouraged, sunshine to the sad, and Nature's best antidote for trouble.

Yet it cannot be bought, begged, borrowed, or stolen, for it is something that is no earthly good to anybody until it is given away!

For nobody needs a smile so much as those who have none left to give!

— Author Unknown

One Heart

If I can stop one heart from breaking,
I shall not live in vain;
If I can ease one life the aching,
Or cool one pain,
Or help one fainting robin
Unto his nest again,
I shall not live in vain.

— Emily Dickinson

Let Me Be a Little Kinder

Let me be a little kinder,
Let me be a little blinder,
To the faults about me
Let me praise a little more.
Let me be when I am weary,
Just a little bit more cheery.
Let me serve a little better
Those that I am striving for.
Let me be a little braver
When temptation bids me waver.
Let me strive a little harder
To be all that I should be.
Let me be a little meeker
To a brother that is weaker,
Let me think more of my neighbor
And a little less of me.

— Anonymous

I Shall Not Pass This Way Again

Through this toilsome world, alas!
Once and only once I pass;
If a kindness I may show,
If a good deed I may do
To a suffering fellowman,
Let me do it while I can.
Not delay, for it is plain
I shall not pass this way again.

— Author Unknown

Drop A Pebble in the Water

Drop a pebble in the water; just a splash, and it is gone;
But there's half-a-hundred ripples circling on and on and on,
Spreading, spreading from the center, flowing on out to the sea.
And there is no way of telling where the end is going to be.
Drop a word of cheer and kindness; just a flash and it is gone;
But there's half-a-hundred ripples circling on and on and on,
Bearing hope and joy and comfort on each splashing, dashing wave
Till you wouldn't believe the volume of the one kind word you gave.
Drop a word of cheer and kindness; in a minute you forget;
But there's gladness still a-swelling, and there's joy a-circling yet,
And you've rolled a wave of comfort whose sweet music can be heard
Over miles and miles of water just by dropping one kind word.

— James W. Foley

CHAPTER TWO

Commitment

SOLUTION

INTRODUCTION FOR PARENTS

"I had no idea she would be there. My apologies for her absence had been well-rehearsed.

When my high school home economics teacher announced that we would be having a formal mother-daughter tea, I felt certain I would not be serving my mother at this special event.

So I will never forget walking into the gaily decorated gym—and there she was! As I looked at her, sitting calmly and smiling, I imagined all the arrangements this remarkable woman must have had to make to be able to be with me for that one hour.

Who was looking after Granny? She was bedridden following a stroke, and Mom had to do everything for her. My three little sisters would be home from school before Mom got there. Who would greet them and look at their papers?

How did she get here? We didn't own a car, and she could not afford a taxi. It was a long walk to get the bus, plus at least five more blocks to the school. And the pretty dress she was wearing, red with tiny white flowers, was just right for the tea. It brought out the silver beginning to show in her dark hair. There was no money for extra clothes, and I knew she had gone into debt again at our coal company store to have it.

I was so proud! I served her tea with a happy, thankful heart, and introduced her boldly to the group when our turn came. I sat with my mother that day, just like the rest of the class, and that was very important to me. The look of love in her eyes told me she understood.

I have never forgotten. One of the promises I made to myself and to my children, as young mothers make promises, was that I would always be there for them. That promise is difficult to keep in today's busy world. But I have an example before me that puts any lame excuses to rest. I just recall again when Mother came to tea."

— Margie H. Coburn

During our lifetime we make many commitments. We commit to being educated and to attend school. We commit our loyalty to friends. We commit to bank loan officers, employers and politicians. However, of all the commitments we make in life, commitment to our family is the most important.

What does being committed to our family mean? I believe it means that we give our hearts and our time to our family, no matter what the consequences may be. We commit to do whatever is necessary to ensure family happiness. There are countless ways to show our commitment to our family. I would like to suggest three things we can do to demonstrate this virtue in our lives.

1. Let family members know without a doubt that we love them. During the years I was a school teacher I taught over 3,000 students. Countless times children would struggle to achieve, fully believing that their parents' love for them was conditional upon their success in school. At first I thought the students were mistaken. Surely parents wouldn't withdraw their love if their child, in spite of his best efforts, did poorly in the classroom. Sadly, too often I was the one mistaken. There were many parents who saw their child's performance at school as a reflection on them and treated the child unkindly when he didn't meet their expectations. These parents gave love only when grades were high, contests were won, and rules were obeyed. That is conditional love.

The issue of conditional love applies to children as well. It is likely that children will be more cheerful, obedient and loving at home when they get things they want and life is "going their way." However, when parents ask those same children to do chores, or give their time to the family when they'd rather be doing something else, how do they respond?

All of us can examine our actions to decide if we show conditional or unconditional love to family members. Unconditional love means that we love the members of our family no matter how they act. We may believe strongly that their actions are wrong, and as parents we should discipline our children for unacceptable behavior. However, unconditional love means that even when we disagree with a person's actions, we still love him. We show that love through our kind (sometimes necessarily firm) tone of voice, and our kind words and actions, even when we are in disagreement.

Family members need to show one another that the basis of their relationship is unconditional love, no strings attached, no matter what. We need to look in our children's, our parents', our brothers' and sisters' eyes and say, "I love you." Often. Family members need to know that love for them does not depend on whether they win the game, drive a fancy car, earn a promotion at work, or anything else. We need to make it very clear to one another that there is nothing we must do to earn love. Nor is there anything we can ever do that will

When we are committed to family

1. We understand that commitment includes fidelity between spouses.
2. We have a unity that puts the family first, but helps promote the well-being of each family member.
3. We tolerate one another's shortcomings and practice patience.
4. We recognize that abuse and abandonment are not options.
5. We seek solutions when problems arise.
6. We celebrate and adapt to inevitable family changes.

C O M M I T M E N T

destroy our love for one another. This does not mean that we aren't grieved when unwise decisions are made. We still need to constantly strive to be the best we can possibly be. But it does mean that we will love one another no matter what happens.

2. Let our family know that we will be there for them. This powerful statement tells family members they are of such immense value that someone is willing to sacrifice for them—to give their very life for them if necessary. Thankfully, we aren't usually called upon to make huge sacrifices for one another. But are day-to-day small sacrifices sometimes difficult? Yes. The following exercise can become part of a discussion on commitment to the family, and sacrifices we each make: Ask your children to talk to Dad about how he feels sometimes at work when he is required to do things that take him to his very limit. Ask Mom what she felt like during her ninth month of pregnancy. Ask children how they feel when they've returned home after a long day at school or work and parents want them to cheerfully do chores instead of relaxing. We all make sacrifices. That's part of what being in a family is all about. We give to one another because we love each other and we believe in our long-term goals of growth, peace and happiness.

Years ago I heard some good advice for parents: "Be there at the crossroads of your children's lives." This means that as often as possible we need to be there when our children come home from school. We need to be there when our children hit their first home run, graduate from school, and when our teenagers need to talk (usually late at night). Time is precious. Time is what lives are made of. We need to be so committed to our children that we are willing to give them our time. Children don't thrive on "leftover time" as well as on "prime time." Even when it is inconvenient, we should be there for our children whenever possible. I'm not saying that we should give to our children at the expense of our own identities. There can be a balance, and we usually know when we are giving too little or too much.

This concept needs to be extended to children also. Children need to understand that families are like teams—they work together to reach the same goals. Children have very important positions on the team and are needed to make it work well. Parents, do you tell your children how important they are to your family's success? Do your children know that you need them to support, appreciate and love you just as much as they need you? Share with your children the idea that as they become adults (and you get old) you may need them just like they needed you as babies. It's called the circle of life.

Love is communicated in many ways. One of the most powerful ways we can show our love is to be there for our family when they need us.

3. Always be honest. Parents and children alike should have an understanding that they will never, ever purposely say something that is not true. When you practice the principle of honesty in your home, then confidence, respect, and trust exist. This works for both parents and children.

Parents, our children will notice any inconsistencies between what we say and the way we live. Our inconsistencies will undermine our credibility. They will also destroy our opportunity to discipline our children, especially in their teenage years, when they begin to question our authority. If we establish a high level of consistency in our words and actions, our children will soon discover that they can count on us to follow through with what we have said, whether that results in something positive or negative. For example, when we tell our child, "If you come home late again, I am going to take away your driving privileges," we must do what we said, even if it is difficult or inconvenient. On the other hand, when we tell our children, "If you clean up your room, I will take you swimming this afternoon," we must keep our promise. Otherwise, our children will quickly realize that our words don't have any real meaning. A broken promise is a lie to a child. Consistent truth-telling on the parents' part sets the ground rules for honesty on the children's part.

As parents we should teach our children that there needs to be consistency in their words and actions. When parents know without a doubt that children are honest, we can trust them and allow them more freedom. When parents know that children will keep their promises, we are more willing to make promises with them. Usually parents trust their children until children lie. Then trust diminishes and is difficult to restore. The fact is that dishonesty damages relationships. Once relationships are broken they can only be repaired by repeated, healing acts of honesty. A good way to show commitment to family is by being honest, always.

Perhaps the greatest value of commitment is that it serves as an expression of love. Love is a concept the experts have trouble defining. But strong families know what love means. It means commitment. It means being there through thick and thin, and it means not giving up when the going gets tough. Commitment is not an easy skill to learn. It requires considerable effort, much practice, and frequent sacrifice. Nonetheless, it is worth it. Commitment to family makes all the difference and guarantees rich rewards.

Commit Your Time

Follow-up

(As a family discuss the assignment for the lesson Kind Actions.)

1. What are some of the ways we are showing more kindness in our family?
2. Can someone share an experience he or she had obeying The Golden Rule? *(Do unto others as you would have others do unto you.)*

Concept

A garden grows well when someone spends time watering and cultivating it. Just like a garden, our family needs us to give our time and effort for it to be successful.

Although our jobs, school, and hobbies are important, our family should be the first priority in our lives. We should be willing to give our family both quality and quantity time.

Quality time means that when we are with one another we are 100% "there," focused on family members' needs and happiness. Quantity time means that we are with our families as often as we can be. This is a challenge sometimes, but when family relationships are truly our highest priority, time needs to be given to those relationships. There is no substitute for unhurried time with our loved ones.

Families are like teams—they work together to reach the same goals. Both parents and children have very important positions on the team and everyone is needed to make it work well. What happens to an athletic team when they don't work together? Usually they don't win. On the other hand, individual players on winning teams are committed to the success of the whole team. They give of themselves, they support and help one another, and they usually do it enthusiastically. Those are good ingredients for a family, also. As we commit our time and hearts to our family, we can reach our goals and "win" in the game of life.

When a person comes to the end of his life, would he reflect on his life saying, "I wish I had spent more time in the office"? Relationships are built on time spent together. Time is precious. It is what lives are made of. Giving our time and hearts to our family shows our love for them.

Family Survey Review

Statement #5. We enjoy doing things together as a family.

- How can we make our family activities more fun?
- Ask yourself silently, "Can I improve my attitude or my support of family activities?"

STORY

Little Kevin ran happily to greet his father when he came home from work. Cheerfully, Kevin exclaimed, "Daddy, I've been waiting for you! I wanted you to come home and read this to me!" Kevin held his book up as high as he could, showing it to his father. John answered his son tiredly, "Yes, I'll read the book to you after dinner."

After dinner John received a telephone call and waved Kevin away with annoyance when Kevin reminded him about the book. After the little boy's bath he found his Dad, who had just sat down to enjoy the evening newspaper. "Daddy, when you finish reading your paper, can you read my book to me?" "Sure, Kevin," was John's reply as he kept his eyes on the newspaper.

An hour later John remembered his promise to Kevin, and hurried up the stairs to his son's room. John found the little boy, fast asleep, with tear-stained cheeks. Kevin's unread book was lying open across his small chest.

Discussion

1. What should the father in the story have done differently?
2. Children, do you ever want your family to spend more time with you?
3. What can we do to give more time to our family?

Activity

For our activity, let's each think of one thing we would really enjoy doing as a family. Let's make a list of all the fun activities we can think of, as many as our family wants.

Now let's decide on one family activity we will do soon. We'll put it on the calendar and plan how to do it. All of us can help plan, and help with the preparations. Then let's DO our family activity.

Assignment

Participate as a family in the three activities that follow this lesson.

1. Family Time
2. Family Dates
3. Commitment Activities

ACTIVITY
FAMILY TIME

Strong families enjoy being together, and they make the effort to plan activities to be with one another. Family time doesn't have to be elaborate or expensive. The simplest activities often become the most memorable. Family time can be as simple as sharing a family joke or enjoying a favorite tradition, such as Saturday morning pancakes or a family walk on Sunday afternoons.

Often when children are asked, "What makes a happy family?" they answer, "Doing things together!" It may seem so obvious that it gets over-looked, but doing things together as a family builds family unity.

Sometimes it's difficult for family members to find the time for family togetherness with work, school, church, and community responsibilities. But the real test of our commitment to our family is the amount of time we spend together. We may have heard that it is quality, not quantity, time spent with children that is important. Since time is at a premium, it is important to spend family "quality time." However, it's also important to spend quantities of time in order to create close relationships with family members. Usually when family members spend time with one another they feel more comfortable sharing their deepest feelings.

Activity—Our Family Time

To begin investing more time together as a family, it's helpful to assess how we now spend our time. We can then decide if that's the way we want to live our lives.

- Take a paper plate and draw lines to divide it into 24 sections for the hours of the day. Divide the plate into thirds, then each third into halves, then each half into fourths. That makes 24 sections.
- Write in the things that absolutely must happen every day. What are those? (*Eating, sleeping, working, going to school.*) Now write in the other things we do each day.

Ask the following questions:

1. Are we spending our time as we wish?
2. How would we like to spend our time?
3. What is preventing us from spending our time as we want?

4. What can we change so that we can spend our time as we would like to? (*Some things we can't change. Concentrate on the things we can change.*)

Ideas for maximizing time together:

- Eat at least one meal together, as a family, every day.
- Take up an exercise that can be shared as a family.
- Work together on household chores rather than assigning separate tasks to each family member.
- Make community service something that will involve several family members, such as coaching a team or being a club leader.
- Turn off the television and play a game. If watching television, discuss the program together.
- Sit by children while they eat breakfast, even if parent skips breakfast.
- Develop the habit of chatting with one another while preparing or cleaning up meals.

Family vacations can be special times that secure family relationships, especially if everyone is involved in the planning and preparation. From planning the vacation to reliving it with pictures and mementos, a family vacation can be an opportunity to reinforce relationships with family members.

A few years from now as we reflect back on the good times with our families, the time we spent together will probably mean more than the remodeled room or new furniture we worked two jobs to be able to afford. Spending time with your family isn't a luxury; it's a necessity.

Activity—Give the Gift of Time

One of the ways we show affection and appreciation is by doing things for people. We also show we care by spending time together. The following activity can help you give your family the gift of time.

1. Decide on something special you will do for someone in your family.

For example:

- Lunch or dinner date
- Car wash
- Help with laundry, homework, yard-work, etc.
- Ice cream cone treat
- Movie or video "date"

2. Decide how often you want to give the "gift" (monthly, weekly, etc.)

3. Make a "credit card" issued in the name of the family member, with a description of your gift. Put a space for them to sign it.

4. Mail it to them in the same way they would receive a new credit card.

5. Each time the card is used, punch or mark it. Make sure the credit card is used and enjoyed.

FAMILY DATES

One of the best gifts we can give our family is time spent together. That does not mean we must do *everything* together. In fact, many times the best "togetherness" is the kind shared one-on-one between parent and child. Finding this time takes planning to fit it into the family's busy schedule. This activity can help parents and children make spending time together a priority. Here are some ideas:

- At the start of each month parents and children schedule a date for spending one-on-one time with each other. If desired, make a Family Date Plan (like the one below) to help organize the dates.
- Mark all family dates on the calendar. Only emergencies can interfere with these dates.
- In two-parent families, Mom and Dad can schedule dates with each other—as well as with the children.

Family Date Plan for _____ and _____
    (Parent)   (Child)

Things we'd like to do	How much time will it take?	Supplies we will need	How much money will it cost?

L E S S O N   S I X

Goals

Follow-up

(As a family discuss the assignment for the lesson Commit Your Time.)

1. What are we doing to give our family more of our time?
2. How have our attitudes been during our family activities?

Concept

A goal is an objective we're trying to reach. Jim Rohn said, "The future does not get better by hope, it gets better by plan. And to plan for the future we need goals." The purpose of goals is to focus our attention on what we want to achieve. We can achieve more individually, and as a family, with clear objectives.

Defining our goals will help point us in the direction we want to go. The great basketball player Michael Jordan said, "I visualized where I wanted to be, what kind of player I wanted to become. I knew exactly where I wanted to go, and I focused on getting there."

Helmut Schmidt remarked, "The tragedy in life doesn't lie in not reaching your goal. The tragedy lies in having no goal to reach. It isn't a calamity to die with dreams unfulfilled, but it is a calamity to not dream. It is not a disgrace not to reach the stars, but it is a disgrace to have no stars to reach for. Not failure, but low aim is the mistake."

An interesting observation was made by Richard Gaylord Briley when he said, "At this very moment you are WHO you are and WHERE you are because of what you've allowed to inhabit your goal-box." It is heart-warming to realize that at any time we can set new goals for ourselves, to improve as individuals and as a family. Tomorrow is the first day of the rest of our lives.

Family Survey Review

Statement #6. We set family goals together.

How did we each respond to this? *(Discuss the Family Survey responses for #6.)*

• How can goals help point us in the direction we want to go as a family?
• How can we help one another reach our goals?

STORY

There was once a farmer who hired a teenage boy to help him do the fall plowing. The boy's first day on the tractor was disastrous. Because he was looking backwards, watching the plow turn the soil behind him, the boy didn't realize until he reached the end of the field that the row was very crooked.

Toward the end of the day the farmer arrived to survey the young man's work. The crooked rows prompted him to give the boy some advice: "You can't plow a straight row if you keep looking back. You must focus your eyes on a goal straight ahead, and move forward toward it—not swerving to the right or to the left—and never look behind you."

So it is with life. Plowing a straight way into the future is powered by goals. Focusing on the past, or what lies behind, will prevent us from effectively pursuing our future goals. Goals help us focus our energy on what lies ahead.

Discussion

1. What is the advice the farmer gave to the teenager?
2. What can we do to keep focused on our goals, as Michael Jordan and the farmer in the story suggested?

Activity

We're now going to have each family member choose three goals—one in each of three areas: physical, mental, and social. Then we'll each list one way to reach our goals. Example:

1. PHYSICAL GOAL: "I want to be stronger. I will lift weights three times a week."
2. MENTAL GOAL: "I want to be smarter. I will read one book each month."
3. SOCIAL GOAL: "I want to be well-liked. I will be kinder to others."

Now we'll set one family goal. Everyone needs to participate and share their ideas about what our goal should be. Here are three examples:

1. "For one week we'll try not to criticize any family member or friend."
2. "We will try to be better neighbors by being friendlier and more helpful."
3. "Our family will try for one month to exercise more regularly and eat more healthful foods."

Assignment

1. Discuss and plan ways you can help each other reach your goals. Then in your family meetings talk about the progress you've made toward your goals. After reaching your goals, congratulate yourself. Then it is time to set new ones, to continue improving your lives.

2. If you wish, read the Additional Solution For Success: Are We Going Where We Think We're Going?

GOALS

ARE WE GOING WHERE WE THINK WE ARE?

Sometimes people spend their resources of time or money on things that bring the least reward in terms of what they really value. Families need to regularly review their goals of what will bring individual and family happiness. Then they need to see if they are spending time doing things that bring them lasting joy. If they aren't happy they need to reevaluate their priorities and actions and have the courage to make changes. If they don't, they may climb the ladder of success only to find that it's leaning against the wrong wall. Too late, families may regret how they spent the years they had together.

To help your family examine what you value most, name things you enjoy doing as a family. Now talk about how often you do the things you really enjoy. Answer these questions:

1. What does our list of things we enjoy doing tell us about what we value most?
2. What does how often we do these things tell us about our priorities?

Despite what you *say,* what you *do* shows how you really feel. What you spend your time doing will show what you really want for your family.

Decide as a family to spend more time doing the things that will strengthen you and make you happy. The following activity will help you look to the future.

Activity

1. Have one person keep time while everyone writes their answers on paper.
2. Everyone answer the following question in three minutes: "How do you want to spend the rest of your life?" Make a list of goals and activities.
3. Answer the second question in three minutes: "What do you want to do in the next five years?" Again, list goals and activities.
4. Answer the third question in three minutes: "If you only had six months to live, how would you spend it?" List activities and goals.
5. Share one another's ideas and talk about how you can help each other reach your goals.

Where the Heart Is

Think long, dear heart,
Before you choose
To what or whom
You give your love,
For God has said
And time has proved
The heart that loves
Grows soon alike
In thought and deed
In soul and sight
To that which it
But treasures most

— William Bagwell

LESSON SEVEN

Service

Follow up

(As a family discuss the assignment for the lesson Goals.)

1. What are the goals we set as a family?
2. What are we doing to reach our goals?

Concept

Service is kindness in action. Service is giving to others—lifting loads and brightening lives. Having an attitude of service means looking for ways to help rather than waiting to be asked. The needs of others are important to those who unselfishly serve. They help people because they care about them, not because they expect a reward. Those who serve others will also benefit—they'll enjoy good feelings of self-worth and an increased capacity to love.

For a child, serving others can be as simple as being friendly at school. One teacher said, "Children who have attitudes of service are alert to situations in which classmates are hurting. If they see a student eating alone, they sit with him. They are understanding and caring."

For a parent, serving children and family is part of the "job." A parent's attitude about service is a powerful example to children. Serving cheerfully teaches children that joy comes from service.

The truth is that "self-centered" people are not as happy as those who are "others-centered."

Instead of looking at mirrors to see what we need, let's look through windows to see other people's needs. In families there are countless opportunities to serve one another.

A Hindu proverb reads, "Help thy brother's boat across, and lo, thy own has reached the shore." Lightening the burdens of others brings joy, and strengthens us individually and as a family.

Family Survey Review

Statement #7. Our family helps one another.

- Do we help one another? What are some of the things we can do in our family to help each other?
- What are some of the ways we can give service without being asked?

STORY

There are two seas in Israel. One sea is fresh. Fish live in it. Trees and bushes grow near it. Children splash and play in it. The river Jordan flows into this sea from the north with sparkling water from the hills. People build their homes near it. Every kind of life is happier because it is there. The same river Jordan flows south out of it into another sea. Here there are no fish, no green things, no children playing, no homes being built. Stale air hangs above its waters, and neither man nor beast will drink of it. What makes the difference between these neighbor seas? Not the Jordan River. It empties the same good water into both. Nor is it the soil or the countryside.

The difference is that the Sea of Galilee receives water but does not keep it. For every drop that flows in, another drop flows out. The giving and the receiving go on in equal measure. The other sea hoards its income. Every drop it gets, it keeps. The Sea of Galilee gives and gives. The other sea gives nothing. It is called the Dead Sea.

There are also two kinds of people in this world—those Dead Sea people who take without giving back, and the givers who remain fresh and vibrant by freely giving service and sharing of themselves.

Discussion

1. Which sea are we like—the Dead Sea or the Sea of Galilee?
2. How can we be more like the Sea of Galilee, giving of ourselves to others?

Activity

As a family, let's participate in one of the acts of service listed below, or think of our own.

- Plant a tree.
- Clean/rake/snow-shovel a neighbor's yard.
- Be friendlier at school.
- Help an elderly person with housework or yard work.
- Tend children for a young mother without pay.
- Read to a child.
- Pick up trash along the highway.
- Do volunteer work in the community.
- Take a meal to a needy family.
- Contribute to church and community projects.

Assignment

1. Keep looking for opportunities to serve others—at home, at work, and in the community.
2. Each family member do one act of service during the coming week. Then, at the next lesson, share what you did.
3. If you wish, as a family do one (or both) of the activities: Taped Books; Form Letter.

TAPED BOOKS

In many families, reading aloud is an enjoyable tradition. Listening to familiar voices and reading favorite stories helps children feel loved and secure. It also helps develop a life-long appreciation for books. Adults benefit, too, because reading aloud to a child provides a chance to spend special time with them.

In today's families, members don't always live together in the same household. However, as the following activity shows, distance doesn't have to interfere with the closeness that comes from reading aloud. Grandparents, aunts and uncles, etc., can still read aloud to younger family members even though they're miles apart. Younger family members can read to elderly relatives also.

Activity

1. Buy or borrow one or two books suitable to the listener's age and interest level.

   Examples:

   For Reading Out Loud! A Guide to Sharing Books with Children, Margaret Mary, Kimmel & Elizabeth Segal, New York: Delacorte Press, 1983.

   The Read Aloud Handbook, Jim Trelease, New York: Penguin Books, 1982.

2. Read the books before making the tape so you are familiar with the story and vocabulary.
3. Now, read the book aloud as you tape.

• First, explain how glad you are to be reading to them.
• Next, give the title and author of the book.
• Read slowly and naturally, as though the listener were sitting beside you.

4. When the tape is filled, mail it (with the book, if you desire) in a padded envelope.

FORM LETTER

Dear _____,

Hello! How are you? We are trying to write more often, and our family thinks using this form letter will help us. You might be interested to know that _____
_____.

It's been really _____because
_____.

The weather here has been

❑ rainy   ❑ sunny   ❑ gorgeous   ❑ windy
❑ snowy   ❑ gloomy   ❑ warm   ❑ heavenly
❑ foggy   ❑ hot   ❑ nasty   ❑ stormy
❑ muddy   ❑ humid   ❑ yucky   ❑ other

and so I have been _____.

Things have been pretty _____ at our house.
_____is/are_____, and that means that
_____. Last week, _____
had to _____
because _____.
_____ says to tell you _____.
He/She is _____ and will probably
_____ before too much longer.

One wonderful / terrible / exciting / interesting thing that happened to me recently was _____.
I felt really _____ about it because _____
_____. Before I go, I just want to say
_____ and I hope you
_____.

Fondly,

LESSON EIGHT

Traditions

Follow-up

(As a family discuss the assignment for the lesson Service.)

1. How are we doing in our efforts to be like the Sea of Galilee—giving of ourselves to others? Has anyone done a service they'd like to tell us about?
2. How did we do with our family service project this month?

Concept

A family tradition is an activity that a family does regularly. Often traditions are so simple that families don't even consciously recognize them as traditions. For example, if a family always has special birthday celebrations, that's a tradition. If they like to eat certain kinds of food on Sundays, that's a tradition. Any activity repeated over and over becomes a tradition, and families share those happy memories. The personalities of families are expressed through the little things they do that add fun to life.

Healthy relationships are built on time spent together. Family traditions create opportunities for us to be with one another. As we join together and participate in a tradition, we share our lives in special ways that are unique to our family. Usually, the more we share our lives, the more we care for one another.

A family is like a chain, and family members are like the links in the chain. Experiences shared together strengthen and bind the links together. The stronger the links, the more powerfully family members are bound to one another. Traditions strengthen family links by giving family members a sense of belonging, something to depend on as they enjoy common activities. Our time together as a family is priceless. The memories we make will last throughout our lifetimes.

Family Survey Review

Statement #8. We have family traditions.

- Why is it important for a family to have traditions?
- What are some of our family traditions?

STORY

One winter a mother took a group of high school students on a night snowshoeing trip to a friend's cabin. The moon was beautiful and full as it shone on the new-fallen snow. For nearly five miles they puffed and plodded along. The first mile or two still held the excitement and mystery of an adventure. But as time wore on, tired legs could scarcely drag nearly frozen toes from drift to drift up the mountainside. The backpacks were no help either. And every few minutes someone's snowshoe straps would come loose or break, sending that person flying into a snowbank head first.

No one complained much, though, because they all knew a warm cabin was waiting at the top.

When the group finally reached the cabin and worked the old door open, they gasped as they looked around. Windows were broken, the kitchen table had three legs and a stump, three rusty springs showed through the upholstery on the couch, and the cabin itself seemed very small. Months before, someone had left the chimney flue open and frozen snow was jammed in the fireplace all the way to the roof. One teenager picked away at the solid block with a pocketknife, while another went to the kitchen to start the wood-burning stove. Disaster again! The stovepipe had separated and was also packed with snow. It was frighteningly cold, and the cabin was quickly filling with the choking smoke. Everyone was complaining and feeling sorry for himself.

"Hey!" the mother who led the group shouted, "There's a new rule. For every complaint you make, you've got to say something good as well." More grumbles. She added, "Well, what have we got to lose? We can at least die with positive attitudes!" Everyone chuckled softly.

"But I'm freezing," one young man complained. The woman smiled and waited patiently. "Uh," he choked, "but at least the smoke is warming the place up."

"Three of the four windows are broken," a girl grumbled. But then she brightened. "At least they draw out the smoke. Should we break the other one?" That brought a real laugh.

As the woman poked in the fire, billows of smoke seeped from every crack in the old stove. She hoped it would melt some of the ice above. After unloading each armload of wood, one pair of students rushed to open the door and draw a few fresh breaths of cold mountain air. Two others alternately fanned the fire and dashed for the door to breathe, while one boy struggled with the broken stovepipe.

Gradually the smoke began to clear. As the snow in the stovepipe melted, the cabin warmed up, and so did their spirits. Before long the campers had a big pot of hot soup on the stove, and the young people were sitting on their rolled-out sleeping bags, happily sipping hot drinks.

Without exception, the memories of that trip are good ones. No one seems to remember the grumbles or the complaints. And the mother who led the group started a new tradition in her family. Whenever some-one has a complaint, he always has to add something positive afterward. She believes this tradition will help her family through any challenge.

Discussion

1. How can this family's new tradition help them through their challenges?
2. If we said something positive after complaining, could it help us?
3. Has our family ever started a tradition without planning it?

Activity

Our activity for this lesson is to decide on a new tradition for our family. Some ideas are listed below. We can use one of these, or think of our own.

- Declare a "Be-Kind-To-(name)-Week." Do something nice for the person every day that week.
- On birthdays, take turns telling the birthday person one reason why you love or appreciate him or her.
- Create a "Memory Wall" in your home, consisting of important events in the family, from school plays to family trips.
- When the family gathers together, play games and enjoy treats.
- Display children's artwork.
- If both parents work, leave a little treat and an envelope for each child containing instructions on what to do during the afternoon.
- Send family members love notes in lunch sacks, desks, on mirrors, etc.

Assignment

1. Plan the details of a new family tradition. Everyone in your family can help with some part of this tradition.
2. Do the activity: Family Scavenger Hunt.
3. Read the Additional Solution for Success: Family Hobby.

FAMILY SCAVENGER HUNT

Many things in our homes have a story behind them, or they're related to a tradition. This activity is intended to help families strengthen their feelings of family pride and history by learning about special family possessions.

Activity

1. Make a list of things you're going to hunt for. Use the Scavenger Hunt List here or make your own.
2. Have family members work individually or in teams. Set a time limit.
3. After the time has expired, gather everyone together to see what they've found. Have each person show the things they found.
4. Talk about each item and explain why it is special to your family.

Scavenger Hunt List

- Find something in your house that used to belong to somebody else.
- Write the name of a food that everyone enjoys having for dinner.
- Count the total number of books you have in your house.
- Write the color of paint, bedspreads, or curtains that you used to have in your house before the current decor.
- Find an object that represents something everyone in your family likes to do together for fun.
- Find something that is older than the oldest person living there.
- Find something that is broken or doesn't work anymore.
- Find something that represents one of your family's special traditions.
- Find something that was bought in another state or foreign country.
- Find a tape, CD, or movie everyone in your family likes.
- Find the oldest photograph you have.
- Find something that reminds you of one of the happiest moments that have occurred in your family.
- If you were moving away and could only take a small 4' x 5' trailer with you, what family possessions would you pack?
- If a flood was coming and you could only save one thing from your house (besides your family), what would you take?

ACTIVITY
FAMILY HOBBY

A hobby is an activity that is done for pleasure. One of the things that make families work well is participating in a hobby as a family. This requires effort on the part of family members, but the more you share your lives, the more you'll enjoy one another.

Have each family member write on a paper what they would like to do for a family hobby. Collect the papers and read them, making only positive remarks about the ideas. Suggestions for possible hobbies:

- Gardening
- Bicycling
- Camping
- Cooking
- Self-defense: taking lessons, competing
- Music: playing musical instruments, attending concerts, etc.
- Hiking
- Collecting things: stamps, antiques, etc.
- Traveling
- Art: drawing, painting, etc.
- Sewing
- Fishing
- Boating
- Woodwork

After all the ideas for a family hobby have been read, discuss what would be the best hobby for your family. You may decide on two or three hobbies!

Choose a family hobby and schedule a day to begin. Discuss what you'll need for your hobby and assign family members to get what is needed. Perhaps you'll want some instruction. If so, contact someone to teach your family about the hobby you've chosen. During your weekly family meeting, schedule dates regularly to participate in your hobby.

SOLUTIONS THROUGH STORIES AND POEMS

COMMITMENT

Determination

Nowadays the four-minute mile is commonplace for champion runners, but at one time it was scarcely thought possible. The man who proved it could be done was the British medical student Roger Bannister—the man with the will to win.

Bannister had been disappointed at his performance in the 1952 Olympic Games and had just about decided to give up on running and concentrate on his medical training. He told his coach this.

"Roger," said his coach, "I think you are the man who can break the four-minute mile. I wish you would give it one last chance before you quit."

Roger went home and thought about this. Before the night was over, he had crystallized in his mind in the form of an iron will the determination that he was going to break the four-minute mile barrier before he quit running.

He knew what he had to do. He would have to study between eight and ten hours a day in order to get through medical school. He would have to train for four hours a day, run to build up his body to peak perfection, go to bed early, sleep nine to ten hours a night so that his body could recuperate—all this to build up for that great day. He was willing to pay this price in addition to his previous training. For several months he went through a routine just like that.

Finally the day came for the four-minute mile. It was a bad day for the competition. It had rained for five hours, and there was a sharp wind blowing, which made it a slow track. But Roger was not deterred. He told his running mates what he was going to try for. They encouraged him, shook his hand, and said they would do what they could to help by pacing him.

The first lap was right on time—57.5 seconds. Because of the slow track, all the runners had to push in order to maintain that pace for the second lap, but when they finished it they were still on time—one minute 58.2 seconds. Then they went into the third lap, the hardest of all. This is when fatigue starts setting in. Roger and his running mates were tired, but at the end of the third lap, they were still on time—3 minutes and 0.5 seconds in all. They were on their way to the first four-minute mile in history.

Roger said afterwards that he had never been so tired in his life as when he started that fourth lap. As he went around that first turn, his steps began to falter and he felt dead. His head was throbbing, his lungs were bursting, and his mind began to say to him, "Slacken up, and just try for a win." But as if in reply, something welled up inside of him and said, "Roger, if you run until you collapse on this track, you are going to make this four-minute mile. If your knees hit this track, you are going to do it. For all these months you have trained, and you've got to." So instead of slacking the pace, he fought off the pain, picked up his knees and began sprinting. Numb and tired as his legs were, he forced them to go.

As he hit the last curve, again his stride began to break. Describing it later, he said that there seemed to be an eternity in those fifty yards to the tape. But he closed his eyes, gritted his teeth, and forced himself to hold stride as he pounded down the stretch. Finally, he took that one last step which broke the tape, and he collapsed into the arms of his coach. His time was 3 minutes 59.4 seconds. Roger Bannister had broken through the four-minute-mile barrier.

— Author Unknown

Boy, We Really Have a Swell Bathroom, Haven't We?

It was a gorgeous October day. My husband, Art, and I were down at the boat landing helping our friend Don drag his skiff up on the beach. Art remarked wistfully that it would be a long time before next summer, when we could all start sailing again. "You folks ought to take up skiing like our family and have fun the year round," Don said.

"Doesn't that get pretty expensive?" I asked.

Don straightened up and smiled. "It's funny," he said. "We live in an old-fashioned house—legs on the tub, that sort of thing. For years we've been saving up to have the bathroom done over. But every winter we take the money out of the bank and go on a couple of family skiing trips. Our oldest boy is in the army now, and he often mentions in his letters what a great time we had on those trips. You know, I can't imagine his writing home, "Boy, we really have a swell bathroom, haven't we?"

— Author Unknown

Everyone Cries, "There Wasn't Time."

Time. It hangs heavy for the bored, eludes the busy, flies by for the young and runs out for the aged.

Time. We talk about it like it's a manufactured commodity that some can afford, others can't; some can reproduce, others waste. We crave it. We curse it. We kill it. We abuse it. Is it a friend? Or an enemy?

I suspect we know very little about it. To know it all, and its potential, perhaps we should view it through a child's eyes.

"When I was young, Daddy was going to throw me up in the air and catch me, and I would giggle until I couldn't giggle anymore, but he had to change the furnace filter, and there wasn't time."

"When I was young, Mama was going to read me a story, and I was going to turn the pages and pretend I could read, but she had to wax the bathroom and there wasn't time."

"When I was young, Daddy was going to come to school and watch me in a play. I was the fourth Wise Man (in case one of the three got sick), but he had an appointment to have his car tuned up, and it took longer than he thought, and there was no time."

"When I was young, Grandma and Grandad were going to come for Christmas to see the expression on my face when I got my first bike, but Grandma didn't know who she could get to feed the dogs and Grandad didn't like the cold weather and besides, they didn't have time."

"When I was young, Mama was going to listen to me read my essay on 'What I Want To Be When I Grow Up,' but she was in the middle of the Monday Night Movie and Gregory Peck was always one of her favorites and there wasn't time."

"When I was older Dad and I were going fishing one weekend, just the two of us, and we were going to pitch a tent and fry fish with the heads on them like they do in the flashlight ads, but at the last minute he had to fertilize the grass and there wasn't time."

"When I was older, the whole family was always going to pose together for our Christmas card, but my brother had ball practice, my sister had her hair up, and Dad was watching the Colts and Mom had to wax the bathroom. There wasn't time."

"When I grew up and left home to be married, I was going to sit down with Mom and Dad and tell them I loved and I would miss them. But Hank (he's my best man and a real clown) was honking the horn in front of the house, so there wasn't time."

— Erma Bombeck

My Friend

I love you not only for what you are, but for what I am when I am with you. I love you not only for what you have made of yourself, but for what you are making of me. I love you for the part of me that you bring out. I love you for putting your hand into my heaped-up heart and passing over all the foolish and frivolous and weak things that you can't help but dimly see there. For drawing out into the light all of the beautiful, radiant belongings that no one else had looked far enough to find.

I love you for ignoring the possibilities of the fool and the weakling in me, and for laying firm hold on the possibilities of the good in me. I love you for closing your eyes to the discords in me, and for adding to the music in me by worshipful listening. I love you because you are helping me to make of the lumber in my life not a tavern, but a temple, and of the word of my every day not a reproach, but a song.

I love you because you have done more than any creed could have done to make me good, and more than any fate could have done to make me happy. You have done it without touch, without a word, without a song. You have done it just by being yourself. Perhaps that is what being a friend means after all.

— Author Unknown

Twelve Guideposts for Living

I will do more than belong—I will participate.

I will do more than care—I will help.

I will do more than believe—I will practice.

I will do more than be fair—I will be kind.

I will do more than forgive—I will forget.

I will do more than dream—I will work.

I will do more than teach—I will inspire.

I will do more than earn—I will enrich.

I will do more than give—I will serve.

I will do more than live—I will grow.

I will do more than be friendly—I will be a friend.

I will do more than be a citizen—I will be a patriot.

— Author Unknown

Be the Best of Whatever You Are

If you can't be a pine on the top of the hill,

Be a scrub in the valley—but be

The best little scrub by the side of the rill;

Be a bush if you can't be a tree.

If you can't be a bush be a bit of the grass,

And some highway happier make;

If you can't be a muskie then just be a bass—

But be the liveliest bass in the lake!

We can't all be captains, we've got to be crew.

There's something for all of us here,

There's big work to do, and there's lesser to do,

And the task you must do is near.

If you can't be a highway then just be a trail,

If you can't be the sun be a star;

It isn't by size that you win or you fail—

Be the best of whatever you are!

— D. Malloch

Which Loved Best?

"I love you, Mother," said Little John;
Then forgetting the work, his cap went on;
And he was off to the garden swing,
Leaving his Mother the wood to bring.
"I love you, Mother," said Rosey Nell
"I love you better than tongue can tell."
Then she teased and pouted full half the day,
Till her Mother rejoiced when she went to play.
"I love you, Mother," said Little Nan.
"Today I'll help you all I can.
How glad I am that school doesn't keep."
So she rocked the baby till it fell asleep.
Then stepping softly, she fetched the broom
And swept the floor and tidied the room.
Busy and happy all day was she,
Useful and helpful as a child can be.
"I love you, Mother," again they all said,
Three little children going to bed.
How do you think that Mother guessed
Which of them really loved her best?

— Anonymous

CHAPTER THREE

Communication

S O L U T I O N

INTRODUCTION FOR PARENTS

Robert was a new employee with his company. Getting established as a successful salesman demanded a great deal of time and energy, both physical and emotional.

"I would sometimes wake up at night," Robert said, "in a cold sweat feeling anxious about whether I would make it as a salesman. I worried about having enough money to make ends meet. Some months I made adequate income and some months I did not.

I was becoming an emotional wreck, but didn't share my feelings with my wife Sherie. I guess because I didn't think it was the macho thing to do. I wanted to appear strong and in control to her. But she wasn't fooled. One evening while we were walking in the park, she said, "Robert, you're feeling pretty uptight about how things are going at work, aren't you?" I told her that I was not tense at all, that everything was okay. She didn't let me off the hook. "Yes, you are worried," she insisted, "and I think it's natural. But I don't like to see you feel this way. Let's talk about it and see if your situation is as bad as it seems, and what we can do to make things better."

At that point I opened up to her and shared all of my frustration and concerns. I felt like a dam had been opened up inside me. I had not talked with anyone about this, and it was a great relief to finally get it out. We talked about ways to cut our expenses and things we could live without.

Then Sherie asked me, "What is the worst thing that could possibly happen?" I answered, "The worst thing is that I would lose my job." Then she reminded me that if I lost my job we would still be able to make it on her income, and her job was very stable. We would have to make some changes, but we could make it.

That talk helped a great deal. My sales gradually increased, and today I'm one of the top salesmen for the company. But that's not the most important part of the story. The most important part is that on that evening years ago Sherie was sensitive enough and interested in me enough to know that I was hurting and needed to talk. She cared enough to start the conversation. As a result of talking through that situation, I felt closer to Sherie than I ever had. I think that established our close bond with each other more than any other single event, and it set the pattern for that type of caring, open communication."

Story from the manual "Celebrating Family Strengths," produced by the University of Oklahoma.

Communication is the process or way we transfer information from one person to another so that it is received and understood. *Received* and *understood* are the key words. We can't call it communication if one person talks and another appears to listen. It is only communication—real communication—if information is received and understood.

In the book *Secrets of Strong Families,* Nick Stinnett and John DeFrain write, "Good communication isn't something that just happens among strong families, they make it happen."

We could say that communication is a two-way street with lots of traffic signs and billboards. To really communicate we have to be able to read the signs as we drive and watch for oncoming traffic. Let's view those two sentences from three angles. First, "Communication is a two-way street." Two or more people need to be involved for communication to exist. If we, as parents, are the only ones talking, and our children are not listening, we are not communicating. There is a saying, "I don't care how much you know until I know how much you care." We need to be sure our children know without a doubt that we love them, and that we truly care about their well-being. Then, with confidence in our love and concern for them, usually our children will more readily listen to us.

Second, I believe that as we communicate with our children they give us "lots of signs and billboards" to both direct us and distract us. What our children say does not always reflect their honest, heart-felt feelings. As parents we need to be constantly "reading the signs" of our children's body

---

Four parts of good communication

1. Listening. Listening strengthens relationships by showing that the listener cares about the person speaking. True listening involves hearing with the heart as well as with the ears.

2. Rephrasing. Rephrasing is restating the basic message in fewer or different words, to be sure you understand the speaker and to let him know you're listening and trying to understand.

3. Probing. Probing encourages the speaker to say more by asking questions. Probing directs the speaker's attention inward to examine his or her feelings and thoughts in more depth. This also shows caring and concern on the part of the listener.

4. Positive Speaking. Positive speaking shows kindness and demonstrates that relationships are valued.

language, the expressions on their faces and their tones of voice. Sometimes we need to listen "between the lines" and try to hear what they are really saying, try to understand how they are honestly feeling. Peter Drucker once said, "The most important thing in communication is to hear what isn't being said."

Third, "We will have to watch for oncoming traffic" could mean that as we talk with our children we should expect occasional negative or hurtful words (oncoming traffic) which they don't really mean, or which they unintentionally communicate badly. Again, we have choices. Three wrong ways we could react to unkind words are to be offended, to "get even" by retaliating, or to stop talking. As parents we have the responsibility to teach our children productive behavior by our example. When the oncoming traffic is heavy and harmful, we should choose to use a communication skill that will prevent a collision, and steer the conversation onto smooth roads. What we say will vary by situation, so it is important to know a variety of good communication skills, and then to be sensitive and creative in our methods.

A key to communicating well with our children is to try to remember what it was like to be a child or young adult. Whether the one to whom you are speaking (or listening) is three, thirteen or twenty-three, try to be that age in your mind while you are communicating. Try to "walk a mile in their shoes" and think about being them, with their life experiences, their needs and desires. Then you will be able to use the understanding from that position, and add it to the wisdom of your adulthood, the result being a wonderful place from which you can communicate with empathy and discernment.

If we can put into practice what we've learned about speaking with kindness, and combine it with sharing our hearts openly, and listening with the intent to understand and help, we are on the road to being able to communicate deeply and effectively. Strong relationships are built not on "surface talk," during which people only discuss the weather or other non-threatening subjects. Usually relationships which stand the test of trials and time are those whose participants are willing to communicate the thoughts and honest feelings of their hearts. By doing so, they risk ridicule and rejection. Nonetheless, these people accept that risk because they cannot be satisfied with anything less than sincere, honest, meaningful relationships.

I believe most parents sincerely desire to have meaningful relationships with their spouses and their children. They want to understand one another's true feelings—the innermost thoughts and desires of family members. Parents often just lack the communication skills that allow this to happen. Perhaps because of the way we were raised we never saw people communicating well; the examples in our lives may have been less than ideal. Again, we have choices. We can choose to begin today to learn the skills of effective communication, and then practice and practice until these methods become "second nature." I can promise you that, with practice, you can feel very comfortable using the four parts of communication suggested on page 103, and comfortable with the communications skills outlined in the lessons that follow.

Learning and strengthening communication skills doesn't mean an end to all problems; it doesn't mean that strong families don't have conflict. They do. Family members get angry with each other, misunderstand one another and sometimes just disagree. But when they communicate they're able to get their differences out in the open where they can talk about them, discuss the problem and come to a satisfactory solution which is agreeable for everyone. That doesn't mean the solution will give all involved exactly what they want, it just means they've reached a common ground on which they can agree.

What are some of the advantages of positive, open communication? Family members who have learned to communicate well with one another have learned to talk and to listen carefully. They know and feel each other's joys and sorrows by sharing their thoughts. They know how to laugh together. They enjoy a sense of humor that brings happiness to their lives. Families who communicate well are able to express openly their feelings, differences, similarities and hopes for the future. They practice positive ways of handling conflict so problems are brought out into the open and discussed, and solutions are found.

Good communication also provides security and safety. People know where they stand in the family, and that contributes to a feeling of well-being.

Sometimes we take family communication for granted. We may think we communicate well just because we're a family or because we spend a good deal of time together. However, most of us can improve our communication skills.

Relationships are built one interaction at a time. Each interaction moves the relationship in a positive or negative way. We usually can't change relationships overnight, but making improvements in our communication skills will always move them in positive directions.

Just a few last thoughts about communication. I have learned that when I do the following things as I communicate with my children, my relationships with them are positive:

- Show unconditional love as I think, speak and act.
- "Be them" for a moment as we talk together. By this I mean to have empathy for their position as I remember what it's like to be young, and try to think like they are thinking, with their life experiences, needs and desires.

> "There may be no single thing more important in our efforts to achieve meaningful work and fulfilling relationships than to learn to practice the art of communication."
> — Max De Pree

• Understand their honest feelings before I try to be understood.
• Listen carefully.
• Speak positively.
• Respond in a way that will be helpful.

Dorothy Nevill made an insightful comment: "The real art of conversation is not to say the right thing in the right place, but to leave unsaid the wrong thing at the tempting moment." Indeed, learning to communicate well is a skill that takes a lifetime.

LESSON NINE

Understand First

Follow-up

(As a family discuss the assignment for the lesson Traditions.)

1. What new tradition did our family start?
2. Do we all enjoy the new tradition? If not, let's talk about how we can make it better.

Concept

Good communication is understanding and being understood. In our family we should be able to talk to one another easily. We should know that we can share our feelings in confidence, know that we won't be laughed at, and feel understood.

Trying to first understand before being understood means that we are more interested in others than in ourselves. It means that we really want to communicate, not just tell how we feel.

We can understand in three ways. First, we think about how the other person is feeling, with their life experiences and needs. We try to "be" that person for a moment. Second, we watch their body language (facial expression, posture) for clues that tell us how they're really feeling. Third, we listen to them very carefully, concentrating on what is being said, not on what we're going to say next.

When we make a real effort to understand before we try to be understood, usually our efforts will be appreciated, our communication will improve, and our relationships will become stronger and more loving.

Family Survey Review

Statement #9. We try to understand one another's feelings.

- Why is it important to understand one another's feelings?
- When people really try to understand you, how does it make you feel?

STORY

To make communication work, we have to understand what people are trying to tell us. Here is a story of a man whom nobody understood.

A construction worker approached the reception desk in a doctor's office. The receptionist asked him why he was there. "I have shingles," he said. She took down his name, address, medical insurance number, and told him to have a seat.

Fifteen minutes later a nurse came out and asked him what he had. "Shingles," he replied. She took down his height, weight, and a complete medical history and told him to wait in the examining room.

A half hour later, a nurse came in and asked him what he had. "Shingles," he replied again. She took his blood pressure and temperature, then told him to take off his clothes and wait for the doctor.

An hour later, the doctor came in and asked him what he had. He said, "Shingles."

The doctor said, "Where?"

He said, "Outside in the truck. Where do you want me to put them?"

Discussion

1. Did the people at the doctor's office assume they knew why the construction worker was there?
2. What could they have done to understand him better?
3. Did the construction worker do a very good job helping the people understand why he was there?
4. What could he have said to be better understood?
5. Are we sometimes like the construction worker in our family by not explaining the details of what we're talking about? Does it cause misunderstandings sometimes?

Activity

This activity teaches how to help people understand us when we communicate. We use "I messages." This is how it works:

"I MESSAGES"	EXAMPLE
1. Start with the word "I."	"I..."
2. Add what you're thinking, feeling or needing.	...need some help getting these dishes done..
3. Explain WHY.	...because I have to leave for work."

Now let's all take a turn. Let's each think of one "I message" to share with the family.

Suggestions:

- "I'm feeling upset when you're late, because we all agreed to be home for dinner at 6:30 each night."
- "I appreciate it when you're on time. It shows me that you care about our rules."
- "I feel angry when you disobey, because you know better."
- "I feel sad when you disobey, because you helped make the family rules."
- "It makes me happy to see you share, because I know you're doing the right thing."

Assignment

The first part of the assignment is to make a real effort to understand people (especially family members) before you try to be understood. Also, read the following: Additonal Communication Skills to Practice.

ADDITIONAL COMMUNICATION SKILLS TO PRACTICE

It's not always WHAT is said, but HOW it's said, that creates happiness or unhappiness.

SAY	DON'T SAY
"I've noticed that sometimes you..."	"You always" or "You never..."
"I feel upset when you..."	"You make me angry when..."
"Help me understand what you're thinking..."	"Why do you..."
"You seem upset..."	"You are angry, so..."
"I'm feeling annoyed when you..."	"I hate it when you..."
"I appreciate it when you do... but it bothers me when you..."	"It bothers me when you..."
"I understand that you're feeling_____, but I'd like to share with you my thoughts..."	"Listen to me!"

You may also participate in the additional activity or read the Additional Solution For Success:

• Who's Who in the Family.
• Communication Skills To Strengthen Family Relationships.

WHO'S WHO IN THE FAMILY

Name_____ Age_____ Sex_____

Position in the Family _____

What do you like about being in this position?_____

_____

_____

What don't you like about being in this position?

_____

_____

_____

What do you like best about yourself? _____

_____

_____

_____

What would you like to change about yourself? _____

_____

_____

_____

What things do you like best about your family?

_____

_____

_____

What things do you wish were different about your family?

_____

_____

_____

Thoughts I would like to share with my family:

_____

_____

_____

COMMUNICATION SKILLS TO STRENGTHEN FAMILY RELATIONSHIPS

- **Communicate and listen:** Focus on attentive listening and "hear" the feelings behind the words. Parents, listen to your children talk about how things are today. Try to see through their eyes and help them see through yours.

- **Affirm and support one another:** Parents, recognize that your role is to guide and influence, and that your child may decide to live differently than you. Allow for differences without withdrawing your love and acceptance.

- **Respect each other:** Show respect for one another's ideas and each person's contributions to the family.

- **Develop trust:** Build a base of friendship and trust with one another. Minimize nagging and yelling; maximize friendly discussion.

- **Have a sense of play and humor:** Set aside time for fun with your family, such as walks, listening to music, playing games together.

- **Share the responsibilities:** Build important skills by having all family members participate in decision-making whenever possible.

- **Teach a sense of right and wrong:** Parents, teach your children by setting good examples for them. Make sure your children play a part in making the family rules and deciding on consequences. One way we gain a sense of right and wrong is by experiencing the consequences of a broken rule.

- **Nurture rituals and traditions:** Find ways family members can feel important and part of the family structure: sharing chores, cooking, helping pay the bills, planning a trip; or simply telling one another what makes them special in your family.

- **Foster family table time and talks:** Begin family meetings where everyone can share their ideas and be heard. Eat dinner without the TV.

- **Admit to and seek help for problems:** Don't hesitate to get help. Families are finding help and alternatives in support groups and local agencies throughout the country.

L E S S O N   T E N

Positive Words

Follow-up

(As a family discuss the assignment for the lesson Understand First.)

1. How are we doing in our efforts to try to understand before we try to be understood?
2. Has someone made progress in this area that they would like to share with the family?

Concept

Communication can be negative (unkind) or positive (kind). When we speak unkindly to one another it destroys the loving atmosphere we want in our home, and it makes family members feel unhappy and unloved. On the other hand, when we speak in a positive and kind way to one another, our family is happier. Those who hear praise, encouragement and loving words usually have good feelings about themselves, and they can more easily be loving and thoughtful to others.

Let's show our appreciation and love to each other by the way we talk.

How we're spoken to often determines how we feel about ourselves. Those feelings, either good or bad, help determine our self-talk. An example of negative self-talk is, "I'm so stupid!" An example of good self-talk is to think, "That's not like me. I usually don't make mistakes like that."

Self-fulfilling prophecies are things people say to us that sometimes affect the way we act. For example, if a child is told, "You'll never be a good athlete!" he may believe it and never improve his athletic skills. On the other hand, positive comments work wonders. For example, when parents say to a child, "You are a very obedient boy!" they encourage obedience by helping the child believe he always obeys. It is so important to speak positively, because people usually become what they are told they are.

Below are some negative and positive comments that can help determine behavior and character.

Negative	Positive
• "You'll probably fight over this new toy."	• "I know you're going to share this new toy because you are sharing children."
• "You are so disobedient!"	• "I'm sure you'll obey right away next time because you usually obey so quickly."
• "It's about time!"	• "Thanks so much."
• "Well, somebody finally gave in!"	• "You're such a peacemaker in our family. Doesn't that make you feel good when you choose the right?"
• "You kids are always quarreling!"	• "It's not like you to quarrel. You usually get along so well."
• "Mom, you never understand me!"	• "Mom, usually you try to understand me. Could you try a little harder to see how I feel about this?"

Family Survey Review

Statement #10. We speak kindly to one another and try not to criticize.

- How does our family generally speak to one another?
- How can we be more positive and less critical of each other?

STORY

In a small Mexican village, a man named Jose had a terrible argument with his son Pedro.

During the argument Jose and Pedro angrily criticized one another and spoke very harshly.

The next day Jose discovered that Pedro's bed was empty. He had run away from home.

Overcome with remorse, Jose knew that his son was the most important thing in his life. He wanted to communicate his feelings to his son. Jose wanted somehow to get a message to Pedro. The father went to the store in the center of town and posted a large sign that read, "Pedro, please come home. I love you. Meet me here tomorrow morning."

The next morning Jose went to the store, where he found five boys named Pedro who had also run away from home. Each boy had answered the call for love, each one hoping it was his father asking him to come home.

Discussion

1. Do we sometimes say things in anger that we don't really mean?
2. We all want to be loved. Name some ways we can communicate love to others.

Activity

For our activity, we're going to change negative statements into positive ones. Let's take turns and do one statement at a time.

- "You are a slow runner!"

- *Example answer:* "With practice you can be a fast runner!"

- "I can't do that.

- *Example answer:* "I'm having trouble with this. I'll try it again."

- "You never agree with me!"

- *Example answer:* "Usually we agree on things. Can you try looking at it this way?"

- "How can you be so stupid?"

- *Example answer:* "You know, I've made that same mistake myself!"

- "I hate you!"

- *Example answer:* "I feel really angry at what you did!"

- "I'm ugly."

- *Example answer:* "I want to look better."

- "Our family can't spell."

- *Example answer:* "Spelling isn't what we're best at, but look at all the words you spelled right!"

- "You can't ever do anything right!"

- *Example answer:* "You usually do this well. Why don't you try it this way...?"

- "Our family doesn't ever have any fun!"

- *Example answer:* "I'd like to have more fun with our family. How about if we...?"

- "Shut up!"

- *Example answer:* "Please be quiet."

Assignment

Choose one or more of the following assignments:

1. Try each day to turn negative comments into positive ones. Remember that any habit is hard to break. Be kind to yourselves and have patience with one another as you try to improve. As you help one another speak more positively, it will be easier to improve. Read the Additional Solution For Success: Positive Speaking.

2. Read Family Storybook.

POSITIVE SPEAKING

Positive speaking shows kindness. It aims at strengthening relationships by building up the other person.

What are the benefits of positive speaking?

1. **You have the opportunity to express yourself.** If you speak in a positive way, people will listen to you more readily. That gives you opportunities to influence people for good.

2. **It helps build a positive self-image.** Speaking positively, giving praise, compliments and words of appreciation are all wonderful ways to build a person's self-image.

3. **It builds trust in a relationship.** Sincere positive speaking tells people you are not trying to manipulate or take advantage of them; it encourages them to trust you.

4. **It encourages cooperation.** Positive speaking encourages cooperation and friendship.

5. **It promotes honest, open communication.** A person will usually open up and speak honestly and frankly with someone who has shown they care by speaking kindly.

Focusing on the positive while speaking to others helps put life and relationships in perspective, especially when things seem to be going badly. It says, "We are in this together and we are going to win."

Marital therapist Richard Stuart believes that uncensored communication may be more than a relationship can bear. We shouldn't say hurtful, unkind things simply because we believe them to be true. Strong families understand this and work toward a type of measured honesty that is kind. Too often people use the excuse "I'm only being honest" to be overly critical. This is destructive to relationships. Be sensitively honest, speak positively and always be kind.

ACTIVITY
FAMILY STORYBOOK

Most people think there's something special about their family, and that feeling strengthens family unity. Family members share good times and bad, ordinary days and special occasions. Every family has a rich store of experiences, traditions, and memories that are meaningful to them. This activity can help you think about some of the things that make your family special.

Activity

1. Explain that everyone who wants to participate can help write and illustrate a special book about the family. Discuss some things family members might write about from the list below, or make up your own ideas.
2. Encourage family members to write as many "stories" as they want. It is a good idea to plan what they want to write about, and even try a rough draft, before copying the final version into the book.
3. Decide on a "deadline" for having all stories ready to put in the book.
4. Encourage family members who enjoy drawing and coloring to illustrate their stories.
5. Include snapshots and photographs where appropriate.
6. Set up a time when everyone can be involved in putting the book together.
7. Once the book has been written, don't stop there. Keep it up-to-date by encouraging family members to add more writing and art from time to time.

Storybook Suggestions

Depending on the ages of the children, suggest that family members consider the following options for telling your family's story.

Preschool and elementary-age children:

• Draw pictures that illustrate what other family members have written.
• Suggest an event that youngsters will be able to remember and tell about. Examples: the funniest thing Mom ever did; the time Dad fell off the sofa; why we love our pet; etc. Have the child dictate his/her description of the event to a parent or older brother or sister. Be sure to copy what is said, word for word.

Elementary school children:

- Describe a family tradition, outing or other event that holds special meaning for you.
- Describe a funny incident or "inside joke" that involves your family.
- Write about your family from the point of view of the family's pet dog or cat.
- Write about yourself—your special hobbies, your favorite things to do, your likes and dislikes.
- Describe something about your family that's different from other families.
- Write about what it's like to be _____ years old.

Older children:

- Describe various aspects of family life (a typical Monday morning; what happens at dinner time; how family chores are divided; etc.)
- Describe the family as if you were writing a special feature about them for a newspaper or magazine.
- Write about why the family's pet is just like another member of the family.
- Describe one of the happiest/saddest/funniest/scariest/most exciting/etc., things that ever happened to the family.
- Write about what it means to be a big brother/sister.
- Describe your earliest memories of younger brothers/sisters.

Parents:

- Write a family history or time-line that includes important dates and milestones in the family's life.
- Describe the different places the family has lived.
- Keep a section for jotting down all those interesting things children say. Keep it up to date.
- Describe what it means to be a parent.
- Write about family members who are no longer living, but will always be remembered in loving ways.

LESSON ELEVEN

Listening

Follow-up

(As a family discuss the assignment for the lesson Positive Words.)

1. How are we improving with using positive words instead of negative ones?
2. Can anyone share an experience he or she had with positive or negative self-talk?

Concept

Listening is more than just hearing words. It is trying to understand a person's message and feelings. When we listen, it shows that we care. Careful listening also increases our empathy for people's feelings. Empathy means to mentally put yourself in the other person's place, so you can better understand that person's thoughts and concerns. Listening with empathy is one of the greatest gifts we can give another person.

When we listen we should:

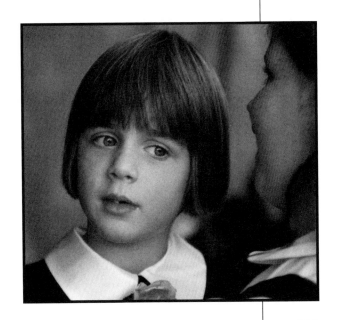

1. **Show we're listening.** We can do this by facing the person, maintaining eye contact, and having an interested facial expression.
2. **Be interested in what the person is saying** and concentrate on the words.
3. **Never interrupt.**
4. **Watch the speaker's body language.** We all communicate much through our facial expressions, posture, etc.

5. **Actively listen.** We should check if we understand by occasionally paraphrasing or repeating what the speaker says. This lets the person know we're listening and interested.

6. **Respond kindly.** When the time is right, we should use empathy as we share our feelings about what has been said, in a way that will help the person.

Listening with love is a virtue we should all desire and seek to acquire. As we listen with open hearts and minds to the messages we hear, we will learn much, and discover how we can best contribute to the happiness of others.

Family Survey Review

Statement #11. We listen to each other.

- Are we good listeners in our family?
- How could we be better?

STORY

This is a story that tells how Thomas Edison, a famous American inventor, made a lot of money simply by using his ears instead of his mouth.

When the Western Union Company offered to buy Thomas Edison's newly invented telegraph ticker, Edison had no idea how much to ask for it. He asked for, and was granted, a few days to think about the purchase price.

Edison and his wife talked about the offer. Although stunned by Mrs. Edison's suggestion to ask for $20,000, he hesitantly agreed and set out to meet Western Union officials.

"What price have you decided on?" the Western Union representative asked.

When Edison attempted to tell him $20,000, the figure stuck to the roof of his mouth. He stood speechless for a moment. Impatient with the silence, the Western Union business person finally blurted, "How about $100,000. for the invention?"

Discussion

1. Did it help Thomas Edison to be silent for a moment instead of speaking when the Western Union buyer wanted to make a deal?
2. Why is it a good idea sometimes to listen instead of jumping in to speak?
3. How do we feel when people listen to us?

Activity

For this activity we need one person to be the speaker and one person to be the listener.

First, the speaker will tell the listener something interesting that happened to him, anytime in his life. The listener should use the six listening skills from the lesson:

1. Show you're listening. (*Face the person, have eye contact, show interest.*)
2. Be interested and concentrate.
3. Don't interrupt.
4. Watch the speaker's body language.
5. Actively listen. (*Paraphrase or repeat what the listener says.*)
6. Respond kindly.

Second, after the speaker finishes, the two participants switch roles and the listener becomes the speaker.

Assignment

Choose one or more of the following assignments:

1. Be more aware of how you listen to others. Help one another improve your listening skills. Here's an example: If you're speaking to a family member who isn't looking at you, say something like, "I sometimes forget too, but do you remember that we're trying to look at each other when we talk and listen?"
2. Do the activity on the following page: Family Oral History.
3. Read the Additional Solution For Success: Listening.

FAMILY ORAL HISTORY

Grandparents, great-grandparents, and older relatives love to talk about their memories. Listening to them helps us understand what their lives were like. It allows us to learn firsthand from their experiences. This is one way to learn why your heritage is so special. In the following activity you'll make a tape recording of older family members to capture the past. It will make a cherished family possession.

Activity

1. Arrange in advance to interview someone in your family.
2. Schedule a time and a quiet place for the interview. Be sure to choose a place where you won't be disturbed by other people, or by background noises that would affect the quality of the tape.
3. Make a list of questions you want to ask. Try to create questions that prompt a story, not ones that can be answered with a simple yes or no.

Sample Questions

A. About you

- What were you like when you were my age?
- What did you do for fun?
- What kind of pets did you have?
- What was it like going to school?
- Where were you born?
- Where did you live? What was your house like?
- Did you have brothers and sisters? Did you get along?
- When did you meet Grandma/Grandpa?
- Do you remember your first date? What was he/she like?
- What were your parents like? What did they do for a living?
- How did you celebrate holidays? What foods did you eat?
- Did your family have any traditions? What were they?

B. About the times

  • Were you ever in a war? Tell me about it.
  • What radio programs did you listen to?
  • Do you remember when you bought your first television set?
  • Did you watch the first astronauts land on the moon?

C. About me

  • When was the first time you ever saw me?
  • What was I like when I was a baby?
  • Am I like my mom/dad when she/he was young?
  • What do you think life will be like when I'm your age?

ADDITIONAL SOLUTION FOR SUCCESS
LISTENING

In the manual "Celebrating Family Strengths," researchers at the University of Oklahoma's Southwest Prevention Center offer valuable information about the skill of listening. They write, "Don't think all listening is something you do just for others. There are some great payoffs for those who listen." Benefits for listeners:

1. You gain knowledge. You can learn a great deal of new information about people and about ideas when you listen. This increases understanding of what is meant, as well as of what is said.

2. Listening stimulates the speaker's expression of ideas and feelings. When you know you are being listened to sincerely and with empathy, you're encouraged to continue speaking and to express your heartfelt ideas and feelings.

3. You become a trusted person. How many times have we heard the statement "to have a friend you must be one?" This applies to families, too. When you listen well you are building trust with the speaker, who feels relaxed, comfortable and secure in your attention.

4. Good listening encourages cooperation from others. When you are genuine in your attention, you encourage others to be genuine as well. Sincere interest in your family members often leads to respect and cooperation. This, in turn, can foster a sharing of ideas and a sense of mutual accomplishment.

5. You can reduce tension and prevent trouble. That can benefit both you and the speaker. Your careful listening gives the other person a chance to "let off steam" before he or she reaches the boiling point. If you learn to listen carefully before you speak, you often can prevent many minor problems before they become major ones.

6. Listening can be fun. Active listening, or listening with your heart as well as your ears, can increase your enjoyment in everything you do. You may actually learn to hear on higher, more positive levels of communication.

Good, effective listening has two key elements:

1. LISTENING AND OBSERVING
2. LETTING THE SPEAKER KNOW THAT YOU ARE LISTENING AND OBSERVING

For many people, learning to listen is difficult. Many societies emphasize speaking, and the other end of the communication is often ignored. Communication is not a one-way street; it requires both speaking and listening.

LESSON TWELVE

Open Communication

Follow-up

(As a family discuss the assignment for the lesson Listening.)

1. What have we been doing to listen more carefully?
2. Can someone share an experience of a family member listening to him or her?

Concept

One characteristic of a strong family is communication that is kind, open, frequent and honest.

Sometimes we expect others to know exactly what we want, or need, even when we say little or nothing at all. Perhaps unkind remarks by others keep us from being open and honest—we're afraid of being hurt or embarrassed. It's very important that family members say only kind, supportive things when someone is sharing their feelings. We should never laugh, or criticize in any way. Instead we should try to understand how the person is feeling, and listen with the intent to help.

When we can say what we really think to supportive family members, good things usually happen:

- We know our family cares about us.
- We believe our opinions and concerns are important.
- Problems are prevented because they are discussed in advance.
- Several people can help find solutions to problems.
- Our family is closer and stronger because we help one another.

In our efforts to be open and honest, we should always remember to be kind. In the name of "honesty" sometimes we can easily hurt feelings, and weaken relationships. In the Disney movie *Bambi,* the rabbit Thumper gives wonderful advice: "If you can't say somethin' nice, don't say nothin' at all."

Family Survey Review

Statement #18. In our family we can say what we really feel.

- Can we say what we really feel in our family?
- What are some of the reasons we don't share our feelings?
- What can we do to help each other "open up"?

STORY

One day not long before the end of World War II, a young man in Germany named Reimund saw two airmen parachuting out of an enemy plane that had been shot down. Like many other curious citizens who had seen the parachutists falling through the afternoon sky, 11-year-old Reimund went to the city's central square to wait for the police to arrive with the prisoners of war. Eventually two policemen arrived with two British prisoners in tow. They would wait in the city square for a car to take the British airmen to a prison where prisoners of war were kept.

When the crowd saw the prisoners, there were angry shouts of "Kill them! Kill them!" No doubt they were thinking of the heavy bombings their city had suffered at the hands of the British. Many of the crowd had come from their fields with pitchforks, shovels and other tools.

Reimund looked at the faces of the British prisoners. They were only 19 or 20 years old. He could see that they were very frightened. He could also see that the two policemen, whose duty it was to protect the prisoners, were no match for the angry crowd.

Reimund knew he had to do something, and he had to do it quickly. He ran to place himself between the prisoners and the crowd. He turned to face the crowd and shouted for them to stop. Not wanting to hurt the boy, the crowd held back for a moment, long enough for Reimund to tell them: "Look at these prisoners. They're young! They are just like your own sons....They're only doing what your sons are doing,...fighting for their country. If your sons were shot down in a foreign country and became prisoners of war, you wouldn't want the people there to kill them. So please don't hurt these soldiers!"

Reimund's fellow townspeople listened in amazement, then shame. Finally, a woman said, "It took a little boy to tell us what is right and what is wrong." The crowd dispersed.

Reimund will never forget the look of tremendous relief and gratitude on the faces of the young British soldiers.

Discussion

1. If you were Reimund, would you have done the same thing he did?
2. Do we speak up at home, school or work for what we know is right or wrong? If no, why don't we speak up?
3. Can anyone tell about a time when he or she spoke up for what was right?

Activity

Family members will all take turns doing this activity. One person asks a question to another family member. The person who answers the question needs to be completely honest, although kind, in his or her response. The two family members should talk to each other in a very open, totally honest way. Listeners should respond only positively. Try to use the skills taught in the lessons on listening and positive words.

1. What is something that happened during the last year which made you happy?
2. What is one thing you dislike about yourself?
3. What is one thing that gets you angry?
4. What is one thing you think our family can do to be happier?
5. What do you think you can do to make our family better?

Assignment

As a family, participate in the following two activities: The Talking Box and Correspondence Activities.

ACTIVITY
THE TALKING BOX

Parents and children need to keep the lines of communication open, but sometimes it's hard to get conversations started, especially when there are important matters to discuss. This activity can help your family talk to one another about important issues.

Activity

1. Set Up

   • Family members prepare the question cards by cutting the questions below from the page and gluing them to index cards. You may want to read the questions ahead of time to see if they are appropriate for the ages of your children. Then put the question cards in the "Talking Box."
   • Encourage family members to add more questions.

2. How To Use the Talking Box

   • Put the box on the table. Allow everyone to choose a question.
   • You can take the box on family outings and trips in the car.
   • The questions can be discussed during bedtime talks.

3. Agree to the Following Rules

   • Family members may not criticize one another for any comment made during Talking Box discussions.
   • If people don't want to answer a question, they may choose another one or pass.
   • No one should be pressured into participating in this activity.

Talking Box Questions

For Parents

   • What is something you really enjoy about being a parent?
   • What day from your childhood would you want to relive?
   • What is something you have learned about life?
   • Describe a time you got really angry at your parents as a child.
   • What is something you did when you were in high school that you hope your children will not do?

• What do you think it is like having you for a parent?

Questions For Teenagers

• What age would you like to be?
• When you have teenage children of your own, what kind of parent do you think you will be?
• Explain why you agree or disagree with the following statement: "School years are the best years of your life."
• Why do you think some teenagers think it's so cool to do drugs?
• What do you think it is like having you for a son/daughter?

For Elementary School Children

• What advice would you give parents about raising children?
• What do most children at your school do at recess time?
• What is something you would like to change about your school?
• Why do you think some children are so mean to others?
• Who is your best friend? Why do you like him/her?
• What do you think it is like having you for a son/daughter?

For Very Young Children

• What do you want to be when you are big?
• What would you do if you could stay up all night?
• If you were the Mommy or Daddy in this family, what would you do when the children act naughty?
• What do you think grown-up people do for fun?

Other Questions

• What is something you worry about?
• Describe something that happened recently that made you really happy.
• Describe something people do that makes you really angry.
• If there was going to be an earthquake tomorrow and your family had to move out of your house, what would you want to take with you?
• If you could spend an afternoon with a famous person (living or dead), who would you choose and why?
• Do you think it is ever right to tell a lie?
• Why do you think some children run away from home?
• Explain your feelings about divorce.
• What do you think happens to people after death?
• Why do you think some people tell jokes about people who belong to different races, religions, or nationalities?

CORRESPONDENCE ACTIVITIES

Friends and relatives who live in other places enjoy hearing about what's happening in our family. However, sometimes the days and weeks go by so quickly that we don't always stay in touch with our relatives. The two activities below are to help families correspond with one another in creative ways.

Activity

1. Address a large envelope to a relative who lives far away.
2. Keep the envelope in a place that is easy to reach (bulletin board or refrigerator).
3. Fill the envelope with the things that reflect what family members have been doing lately:

   • Completed homework assignments and quizzes
   • Drawings, pages from coloring books, and other "original art"
   • Notes from teachers
   • Programs, agendas, or schedules from meetings, music recitals, concerts, school plays and other events
   • Ticket stubs
   • Newspaper clippings
   • Recipes
   • Photos

If necessary, write a note on items to explain them.

4. After a week, or when the envelope is filled, mail it to a relative.
5. Address a new envelope to another family member and start again.

The following activity is designed to help your family get into the letter-writing habit, so you can stay close to loved ones.

Activity

1. Assemble the following supplies in a box: paper, pens, pencils, envelopes, stamps.
2. Talk to your family about why it is important to write to friends and relatives.

3. Explain that any time someone has a letter to write, all the supplies can be found in one place. Always keep the writing supplies in the box so you won't have to hunt for them.
4. Consider setting aside half an hour each month for a family "write-in." Everybody chooses a different relative or friend to write to. Then all letters are passed around the table for everyone to add a short note.
5. Family members who cannot think of anything to say can use the form letter included after lesson seven.
6. Replenish supplies and stamps on a regular basis.

COMMUNICATION

Communicate By Example

Michael J. Dowling was a young man who fell from a wagon in a blizzard in Michigan when he was fourteen years of age. Before his parents discovered that he had fallen from the rear of the wagon, he had been frostbitten. His right leg was amputated almost to the hip, his left leg above the knee; his right arm was amputated; his left hand was amputated; Not much future for a lad like that was there? Do you know what he did? He went to the board of county commissioners, and he told them that if they would educate him he would pay back every penny.

During World War I, Mr. Dowling, who was at the time president of one of the largest banks in St. Paul, went to Europe to visit the soldiers–to visit those who were wounded. On one occasion, he was in a large hotel in London, and he had before him the wounded soldiers in their wheelchairs. They were in a lobby, and he was up on the mezzanine floor. As he started to speak, he minimized the seriousness of their wounds—the fact that one had lost an eye, another had lost an arm, etc. was no grounds for complaint. And he got these fellows so wrought up that they started to boo him. Then he walked over to the stairway and down the stairs toward the lobby, telling them as he walked how fortunate they were, and they continued booing.

Finally, he sat down on one of the steps and took off his right leg. And he kept on talking and telling them how well off they were. Well, they calmed down a little bit, but they still resented his remarks. Then he took off his left leg. Well, the booing stopped then. But before he arrived at the bottom of the stairs, he had taken off his right arm and flipped off his left hand, and there he sat–just the stump of a body.

Michael Dowling was the president of one of the biggest banks in St. Paul. He had married and was the father of five children. He finally died as the result of the strength he gave in encouraging the wounded soldiers of World War I.

— Matthew Cowley

"If you treat a man as he is, he will remain as he his, but if you treat him as if he were what he ought to be, and could be, he will become what he ought to be, and should be."

— Goethe

Thoughts

A few months after moving to a small town a woman complained to a neighbor about the poor service at the local drugstore. She hoped her new acquaintance would repeat her complaint to the owner.

The next time she went to the drugstore, the druggist greeted her with a big smile and told her how happy he was to see her again. He said he hoped she liked their town and to please let him know if there was anything he could do to help her and her husband get settled. He then filled her order promptly and efficiently.

Later the woman reported the miraculous change to her friend. "I suppose you told the druggist how poor I thought the service was?" she asked.

"Well, no," the woman said. In fact–and I hope you don't mind–I told him you were amazed at the way he had built up this small-town drugstore, and that you thought it was one of the best run drugstores you'd ever seen."

— Author Unknown

A smile is a light in the window of the soul, indicating that the heart is at home.

— Author Unknown

I Love You

I love you for the happiness
You bring me each day,
I love you for the kindness
Of your always thoughtful way.
I love you for the tenderness
That lies within your heart.
I love you for the way you say

"I'll miss you when we part."
I love you for the patience
When I do something wrong.
I love you for the laughter
That lingers like a song.
I love you for the gentle way
You cheer me when I'm sad.
I love you for the little things
You do to make me glad.
I love you for the faith and strength
That you have given me.
I love you for the beauty
That you help me to see.
I love you for your love for me,
So constant and so true—
But most of all I love you
Just because you're you!!

     — Author Unknown

The Man with the Friendly Smile

A laugh is just like sunshine,
It freshens all the day,
It tips the peak of life when light,
And drives the clouds away;
The soul grows glad that bears it,
And feels its courage strong;
A laugh is just like sunshine
For cheering folks along.
A laugh is just like music,
It lingers in the heart,
And where its melody is heard,
The ills of life depart;
And happy thoughts come crowding
Its joyful notes to greet;
A laugh is just like music
For making living sweet.

     — Anonymous

It Shows In Your Face

You don't have to tell how you live each day;
You don't have to say if you work or you play;
A tried, true barometer serves in the place,
However you live it will show in your face.

The false, the deceit that you bear in your heart
Will not stay inside where it first got a start;
For sinew and blood are a thin veil of lace
What you wear in your heart, you wear in your face.

If your life is unselfish, if for others you live–
For not what you get, but how much you can give,
If you live close to the Lord in His infinite grace,
You don't have to tell it, it shows in your face.

— Author Unknown

Scatter Sunshine

Oh, scatter sunshine as you go
In all you say and do;
The love and kindness which you show
Will come right back to you!
There is an unseen register
Where all your deeds are filled;
The times you stopped to lend a hand,
The times you paused and smiled.

The times you spoke a fitting word
Of joy and comfort, too;
The times you went the second mile
Some gracious deed to do;

The times you quietly withstood
An enemy's sharp blow,
The times you opened wide your heart
And let the merry flow;
The ways in which you remembered
Some token small to share;

The times you took a moment out
To breathe a silent prayer;

Like homing pigeons they'll return
To bring you gladness, too—
These rays of sunshine, warm and bright
Will come right back to you!

— Lois Rasmussen

Keys

Hearts, like doors, will open with ease
Two very, very little keys;
And don't forget that two of these
Are "I thank you" and "If you please."

— Author Unknown

I Know Something Good about You

Wouldn't this old world be better
If the folks we meet would say,
"I know something good about you!"
And then treat us just that way?
Wouldn't it be fine and dandy
If each handclasp warm and true
Carried with it this assurance,
"I know something good about you!"

Wouldn't life be lots more happy
If the good that's in us all
Were the only thing about us
That folks bothered to recall?
Wouldn't life be lots more happy
If we praised the good we see?
For there's such a lot of goodness
In the worst of you and me.

Wouldn't it be nice to practice
That fine way of thinking, too?
You know something good about me!
I know something good about you!
— Author Unknown

Smile

It's easy enough to be pleasant
When life flows like a song
But the man worthwhile
Is the man who can smile
When everything goes dead wrong
For the test of the heart is trouble
And it always comes with the years
And the smile that is worth the praises of earth
Is the smile that shines through tears.

It's easy enough to be virtuous
When nothing tempts you to stay
When without or within no voice of sin
Is luring your soul away
But it's only a negative virtue
Until it is tried by fire
And the life that is worth the honor of earth
Is the life that resists desire.

By the cynic, the sad, the fallen
Who had no strength for the strife
The world's highway is cumbered today
They make up the item of life
But the virtue that conquers passion
And sorrow that hides in a smile
It is these that are worth the homage of earth
For we find them but once in awhile.
— Ella Wheeler Wilcox

CHAPTER FOUR

Choices

SOLUTION

INTRODUCTION FOR PARENTS

A father from Wisconsin showed special insight when he spoke about choices he made:

"Sometimes in the scrambled schedule of life I get to feeling like the time I spend with my sons could better be spent on work. And then I remind myself that the budget request or schedule of who works when or the productivity report will affect life for a few days or weeks. I have to do it and it is somewhat important—but my job as a father is most important. If I'm a good father to my sons they are likely to be good fathers, too. Someday after I'm gone, and certainly after those reports have rotted, a grandchild or great-grandchild of mine will have a good father or mother because I was a good father. It's kind of a chain reaction."

A businessman from Oklahoma made some wise choices:

"I used to worry a lot; in my business it's easy to do. It got to the point it was about to break me. Then somehow a very important thing happened to me, and I don't know exactly how it happened. I finally realized deep within myself that it was not possible for me to control every little aspect of my life as well as the lives of others, as I had been trying to do. I decided that I could do the best that I could do, but then I had to let go. I had to trust more in other people and in life. I can't do everything on my own, I can't carry the world on my shoulders. This realization gave me an indescribable feeling of relief. Now I'm a much more relaxed, effective and productive person."

Every person and every family has problems. The choices we make as to how we deal with our problems largely determine our happiness or unhappiness. No matter how devastating our circumstances, we can still choose how we think and how we perceive life. Included in the lesson on responsibility is Eleanor Roosevelt's famous quote, "No one can offend me without my permission." We can choose how we react to our circumstances, our environment, and the people around us. Choice is powerful and truly a gift. Even as I write that statement I fully understand that many, many choices in our lives are beyond our control. However, the choice of attitude is always ours.

Problems can be a gift. They provide opportunities to use our strengths, help us appreciate the good times, and help families grow closer together. How we perceive and deal with our challenges involves significant choices.

Entrepreneur Zig Ziglar said, "You are free to choose, but the choices you make today will determine what you will have, be, and do in the tomorrow of your life."

Individuals and families occasionally need to take a "time out" and evaluate their life choices. Sometimes at first our decisions seem to be good ones, but experience teaches us we were wrong. Usually, we have choices as to how we can "get back on course" with our lives. Often, however, these choices are difficult, even when we know they are best for our family. Sometimes I have seen parents choose to continue on destructive courses because it was too much effort to make the needed changes.

More frequently than we realize, our choices produce a ripple effect and alter the lives of others. Let me share an example of the ripple effect caused by a decision made in our family. After my husband Gil had taught high school for fifteen years, he became unhappy with his career course. He wanted to teach at a university. To earn the necessary Ph.D. required to be a university professor, Gil needed to go back to college for an additional four years. Unfortunately, the closest university was two and one-half hours away from our home. So Gil lived in a little attic room near the University of Washington during the week and returned home only on weekends. At that time we had six children, ages 3, 5, 7, 9, 11, and 13. This was not an easy choice. It wasn't long before the full impact of the ripple effect, caused by this choice, was felt in many lives. After years of being a stay-at-home mom, I returned to school teaching. Our children learned to get along without a full-time dad, and it gave them empathy for those with similar circumstances. My parents, Wendell and Gwen Noble, respected Gil's choice and moved 2,000 miles to be near us and help during this challenge. They were with us for three years. Additionally, Gil's parents, Warren and Marian Fellingham, assisted us during this time.

Gil's choice resulted in an entire family effort. Some of the consequences? Well, it was a very long four years. We often got discouraged and impatient with the hurdles we encountered. Frequently we had to refocus on our goal to make it through the long days of family separation. However, the positive consequences of Gil's choice to earn a Ph.D. are many. I learned to appreciate and empathize with single mothers; the children have close relationships with their grandparents because of time spent together; as a family we pulled together and endured to the end of a challenging time; Gil now has doctorate in biostatistics and is teaching at the university of his choice. He

---

Ideas for Dealing with Problems

1. **Focus on the positive.** Try to learn something positive from each challenge.
2. **Maintain open channels of communication.** Listen to and consider the feelings of all the family members.
3. **Pull together as a family.** When you work together as a team, everyone is successful.
4. **Stay flexible.** Flexibility is the key for families coping with change.
5. **Draw on spiritual resources.** A belief in God sustains a family through crisis.
6. **Seek help outside the family.** Look to other relations for help, and be there when they need you.

absolutely loves his job, and he has a great appreciation for the sacrifices made on his behalf.

All choices have consequences. Sometimes the results of our choices are good, and sometimes the consequences are negative, even devastating. I suggest that before making choices, whenever possible, we follow these seven steps:

1. **Study all possibilities.** Research, if necessary, all possible "angles" of the choice, taking whatever time is needed to make the correct decision.
2. **Don't make rush decisions,** especially on life-changing choices.
3. **Discuss your thoughts** with family members and trusted friends.
4. **Keep an open mind** and sincerely consider all of the possibilities.
5. **Pray about your decision.**
6. **Make your choice.**
7. **If, after your best efforts, your choice was not ideal, don't regret it.** Perhaps you could think this: "I made the best decision I could with the information I had at the time." Then go on with your life.

Agency is a God-given gift. How we use our agency in this life is usually our choice.

Responsibility

Follow-up

(As a family discuss the assignment for the lesson Open Communication.)

1. Have we been sharing our feelings in a more open way to family members? How? When?
2. How have we been more kind and understanding when family members try to communicate openly and honestly?

Concept

One of the most important things we can learn in this life is to take responsibility for our own thoughts, words and actions. An American president's wife, Eleanor Roosevelt, spoke about this when she said, "No one can offend me without my permission." We can choose what we think and how we act.

When we take responsibility for our thoughts, words and actions, we don't let other people make us angry. We wouldn't say, "You make me angry!" because no one makes us angry. We can choose to be in control of our emotions.

When we're responsible, we no longer blame others, the weather or our memory.

For example, we wouldn't say things like, "It's not my fault, I forgot!" If something goes wrong,

we can explain, but we make no excuses. If we make a mistake, we take responsibility for it. We admit when we're wrong.

Linda Kavelin Papov, in her book *The Family Virtues Guide,* described responsibility well: "Being responsible means that others can depend on you. Being responsible means to do something well and to the best of your ability. Being responsible is being willing to be accountable for what you do or don't do. You accept credit when you do things right (humbly, of course!) and accept correction when things go wrong. When you are responsible, you keep your agreements. If you agree to do something for your family or for a friend, you don't put it off or forget about it. You make sure it gets done. Being responsible is the ability to respond ably."

Additionally, children learn responsibility by doing as much as possible for themselves. As young children accomplish even the smallest things, older children and parents should praise them and their ability to do things for themselves. Parents, the fewer things we do for our children, the more time we'll have to do things with them.

Family Survey Review

Statement #13. We take responsibility for our own mistakes.

- When something goes wrong, is it easy to blame others?
- Instead of blaming others, what should we say and do?

STORY

Just over the six-foot fence in Jason's backyard was a parking lot for an apartment building. Someone had tossed a paper bag of empty beer bottles from the parking lot over the fence into Jason's backyard where he had found them. Jason took the bottles and tossed them, one by one, back over the fence. Since he couldn't see through the fence, he couldn't see them land, but he could hear the crash each time a bottle broke in the parking lot. It was kind of fun.

That evening a man from the apartments rang the doorbell, and Jason, who was downstairs, overheard the man telling his father about a punctured tire. Jason went quietly into his room, quickly put on his pajamas, got in bed, and pretended to be asleep.

His parents, after reassuring the neighbor they would pay for the tire if it turned out to be their son's doing, sat down to decide how to handle the incident. They realized that they had three challenges: (1)

to help Jason tell the truth about the matter (they knew him well enough to be pretty sure what the truth was); (2) to help him feel sorry for what he'd done; and (3) to help him feel enough responsibility for his actions that he wouldn't do something similarly irresponsible in the future. As they thought about it, they realized that it was fortunate the whole thing had come to their attention after Jason was in bed when they had time to think it through, rather than in his presence. Otherwise they might have confronted him without turning it into a learning experience.

When Jason came to breakfast the next morning, Dad said, "Son, I noticed that sack of beer bottles. Whoever tossed them into our yard shouldn't have done it, should he?"

Jason looked up with a little hope in his eyes and answered, "No."

Dad said, "You probably felt like tossing them back over and didn't really stop to think that they might hurt someone or break something." Jason looked down, but said nothing. "Did you throw them over, son?"

There was a pause, then a quiet, "Yes."

"We're proud of you for telling the truth, son. A man's car ran over one of those bottles and got a flat tire. We're lucky none of the bottles broke a windshield. But we do need to decide what to do about that flat tire. Do you feel sorry about throwing those bottles and puncturing the tire?"

"Yes."

"Are you going to take responsibility for what you did?"

"Yes."

Jason cleaned up the rest of the glass. He saved money from working for three weeks to pay for the tire. He apologized to the car's owner. He promised both his parents and the car owner that he would never throw anything over the fence again. Jason made restitution and took responsibility for his actions.

Discussion

1. How did Jason take responsibility for his actions?
2. How do we feel when we take responsibility for our words and actions?

Activity

First, we'll answer the following questions. They'll help us realize that our daily decisions show how responsible we are.

Ask:

1. What would you do if you broke something in our home?
2. What if you had a family job to do, and your friend asked you to go swimming?
3. What if your teacher gave you a math assignment that you didn't understand, and it was to be finished the next day. What would you do?
4. What if you were tending a neighbor's child who was in the bathtub when the phone rang?

Second, we'll do one (or both) of the activities on the following pages:
1. Ten-Minute Pick-Up
2. The Honey-Do Jar

Assignment

1. During the coming weeks make a special effort to take responsibility for your own thoughts, words and actions.
2. Read the Additional Solution for Success included with this lesson: Learning To Make Responsible Decisions.

ACTIVITY

THE TEN-MINUTE PICK-UP

All family members have a responsibility to keep the home clean. The following activity is a fun way for family members to combine their energies, get household chores done faster, and feel good about doing their part.

Activity

1. Assign family members to "work stations" (areas of the house that need cleaning).
2. Be sure everyone has what they need for cleaning—vacuum cleaner, broom, sponge, etc.
3. Set the timer for 10 or 15 minutes and shout, "On your mark, get set, CLEAN!"
4. Family members are to work quickly and efficiently at their stations to get as much done as possible before the buzzer goes off. If someone finishes early, he or she should run to another station and help someone else.
5. As soon as time is up, allow a few moments for any last-minute cleaning. Then stand back and join in a round of applause for everyone who helped accomplish a marvelous job in such a short time!

HONEY-DO JAR

Dividing household chores among all family members is a good way for children to learn responsibility. This activity guarantees that children will have a chance to do every chore at least once. This is a fair way to distribute housekeeping responsibilities and a good way to prepare children to be on their own someday.

1. Schedule a family meeting to:

• Make a list of chores (inside and out) that family members can do.
• Put a "D" next to daily chores.
• Put a "W" next to weekly chores.
• Put an "M" next to monthly chores.

2. Cut construction paper into "chore" strips. Write one chore per strip as follows:

• Red strips have daily chores.
• Green strips have weekly chores.
• Blue strips have monthly chores.

3. Put chore strips into the "Honey-Do" jar.
4. Decide how many chore strips, and what color, each family member should draw. These decisions will be determined by family members' ages and abilities.
5. Have family members draw from the Honey-Do jar at the beginning of every month.
6. Make sure that the more time-consuming and strenuous chores are distributed fairly.
7. Make a separate Honey-Do jar filled with easier tasks for very young children, like folding towels, pulling weeds, picking up toys.
8. For one month, family members perform the chores they drew from the jar. Repeat the drawing each month.

LEARNING TO MAKE RESPONSIBLE DECISIONS

One of the most important skills to teach in the home is how to make decisions. Children learn this best in families when they have many opportunities to make decisions and when parents explain the reasons for their decisions.

Making decisions is a fundamental skill that is important throughout life. Young people who haven't made decisions about who they are and what they want to do in life are the most vulnerable to peer pressure. Inexperienced decision-makers are more likely to rely on others to make their decisions and define their values for them. On the other hand, those who make many decisions as they're growing up are usually more capable of making choices that will result in their happiness and growth.

Decision-making can, and should, be encouraged by parents from a fairly early point in childhood. Young children can't make many decisions alone because they don't have the experience to avoid safety hazards, to always act in their own best interest, or decide within a value system. Parents can, however, let them make "choices within limits." Parents can say, "You can't play in the street, but you can play in the backyard or in the house. Which would you like to do?" Or, "It's almost time for bed. Would you rather get ready for bed now and then read until it's sleep time, or would you like to play a board game and then get ready for bed?"

It's important that when parents offer choices there really is a choice for the child. Avoid saying things like, "Do you want to get ready for dinner?" when you really mean, "Get ready for dinner now." Don't imply that a choice exists when it really doesn't.

The same idea of decisions within limits can be used as children get older. As children grow, they can be given more and more responsibility and greater opportunity to make their own decisions. Of course, the decisions will still be within parental limits. Choices about clothes to wear, when to do homework, or how to spend allowance can be increasingly turned over to school-age children. It is important for parents to be supportive of their children's efforts to make decisions. Doing so will increase a child's confidence in his ability to make good decisions.

At times, children make choices that parents know beforehand will not work. Sometimes, however, letting children experience for themselves the consequences of their decisions will be a better teacher than parental advice or authority. Helping children consider alternatives that they haven't considered, then standing back while the child decides, is one of the fine arts of parenting.

Suppose we wanted to take a trip. What would be the best way to get there? Choosing a route is a lot like the process we go through when we make a decision. We should consider many possible routes or solutions. Next, we should look at the benefits and costs of each alternative way: time, comfort, cost, scenery, etc. We will then be able to choose the route that will best meet our needs. Similarly, when we make any meaningful decision we should consider several solutions, then make our best choice based on the information we have. There are usually a number of ways we can accomplish things. Making good decisions is the process of identifying the one way that will work best for us.

Finally, after we've given all possible solutions careful thought, and we've made our best decision, we should not look back with regret. Later, if our decision proves to be the wrong one, we should remember that we made the best decision we could, with the information we had at the time.

The Decision-Making Process

1. Identify the problem.
2. List all possible solutions.
3. Think about each alternative—applying your knowledge, values, resources, and the ease or difficulty of the solution.
4. Discuss the issue with those who care about your welfare and happiness. For some this will include God.
5. Choose the best solution.

Keep in mind that decision-making doesn't mean that there is one universal "right" choice for most issues. Different people choose different ways to solve problems that can be equally successful.

Activity

We'll each choose one of the problem situations below. After thinking about the five steps of decision-making listed above, make a decision about what you would do in these situations, and tell why you wouldd solve the problem that way.

Problem 1: Friday night is the big game with your school's rival school. It is also your cousin's wedding. You want to go to both. What should you do?

Problem 2: You have $25. You see the perfect sweater and you want it. Your mother's birthday is next week. You don't have enough money to buy a gift and the sweater. What should you do?

Problem 3: You have been asked to join the track team for spring season. You also want to be in the school play. Both play rehearsal and team practice are after school. What should you do?

Family members are more likely to include one another in their important decisions if they are listened to and feel as if their family cares. Criticizing a family member's decision-making efforts weakens relationships and prevents good communication.

As children grow older and mature, they need to take more and more responsibility for their own decisions. In decisions about college, careers, military service, or even marriage, the primary responsibility ultimately belongs to the young person. A parent can become a trusted advisor and facilitator, helping to locate resources and information so the young person can make informed decisions.

In most families, children grow to young adulthood making decisions that are generally in harmony with their parents' beliefs and values. Sometimes children will choose otherwise. It is a challenge for parents to continue to accept, support and love their child despite their differences. However, loving unconditionally will enable a rich relationship to continue throughout adulthood for both parent and child.

LESSON FOURTEEN

Rules and Consequences

Follow-up

(As a family discuss the assignment for the lesson Responsibility.)

1. How have we improved in our efforts to take responsibility for our own thoughts, words and actions?
2. Do we blame others less?
3. Are we eliminating excuses? Can anyone tell us about a time he didn't make an excuse for something he did wrong?

Concept

In life there are rules—at home, at school and in the community. It's important to have rules in a family for order and peace to exist. When all family members help make the rules, children take the responsibility of helping to set their own limits. Families should gather together and decide on family rules. Then the rules need to be obeyed by all family members.

A consequence is what happens as a result of a choice. When rules are obeyed, good consequences usually follow. When rules are disobeyed, unpleasant consequences follow.

After creating family rules, everyone can decide on the consequences for disobedience. To best change behavior, whenever possible, the consequence should relate to the rule that was disobeyed.

Example: Child disobeys and returns home late after dinner is over. Possible consequences are that he fixes his own dinner, or waits until morning to eat.

Example: Child forgets to take his homework to school. A possible consequence is that he receives a lower grade, then he does extra-credit work to raise his grade.

Consequences can be used inappropriately. For example, if a student's grades are unacceptable, and the consequence is removal from the one school activity that the student likes, then he may have even less desire to go to school. It would be more appropriate to have the consequence for falling grades be extra study time in the evening, under parental supervision. When deciding on rules and consequences as a family, be careful to make them reasonable and do-able.

When children help create family rules and consequences, when they disobey, they are disobeying rules they once agreed upon. Then parents can simply empathize with their children's bad decisions, and remind them of the previously agreed upon consequence which they'll now experience because of the wrong choices they made.

When it becomes necessary for parents to enforce rules and consequences, it is best to be kind and firm at the same time. Gentle words and loving actions show kindness. Consistent follow-through with appropriate consequences shows firmness. An example of firmness: "I'm willing to have Jerry stay overnight only if both of you agree to go to bed by 10 o'clock." There needs to be appropriate follow-through if the children disobey. This could mean that the parents take Jerry home or he isn't allowed to spend the night again.

It is important to understand that obedience to rules prepares family members for life outside the home, and obedience will bring a greater measure of peace and happiness inside the home.

Family Survey Review

Statement #14. We all help make the rules in our family.

- Children, do you like the idea of helping to make the rules?
- Will it will be easier to obey rules that you helped make? Why?
- What should consequences teach us?

STORY

The Canadian Northlands have only two seasons: winter and July. As the back roads begin to thaw, they become muddy, and vehicles traveling through the back country leave deep ruts. The ground freezes hard during the winter months, and the highway ruts become a part of the traveling challenges. For vehicles entering this undeveloped area during the winter, there is a sign which reads, "Driver, please choose carefully which rut you drive in, because you'll be in it for the next 20 miles."

Choose carefully the path your life takes. Once you choose, your choices often will control you. It will be difficult to get out of your "ruts." There are consequences in life for the choices we make.

Discussion

1. What are some rules at school? At work? In the community?
2. What happens when those rules are broken?
3. Are people usually happier when they obey the rules?

Activity

With everyone helping, we're going to create some family rules. Then we'll decide on consequences for obedience or disobedience to the rules.

- Have one person write down all ideas suggested.
- Everyone should have a chance to share his or her ideas about what would be good rules for your family.
- Remember to keep your rules few and simple.

Example: One family member may say, "I think we should have a rule of no hitting in our family." We'll write that down. Then someone might say, "We should each keep our bedroom clean." We will get everyone's ideas for rules. Then we'll talk about which ideas should become our family rules.

Now let's make a list of our family rules and display them somewhere in our home.

Then let's discuss the consequences for obeying our family rules.

Example: The consequence for not hitting one another is helping to create peace and a loving atmosphere in our home.

A consequence for keeping bedrooms clean is a tidy home that contributes to family peace, order and well-being.

Next, let's decide on the consequences for disobeying the rules.

Example: A consequence for hitting would be to apologize, then go away from the family for a few minutes to think about being kind next time.

A possible consequence for not keeping a bedroom clean is staying in the messy room and not participating in enjoyable activities until the room is clean.

Assignment

1. Make a real effort to obey your family rules and to have good attitudes when dealing with a consequence. Parents, try to be loving, firm and consistent.
2. Read the Additional Solution For Success: Family Values.

ACTIVITY

FAMILY VALUES

Each of us lives by a set of values that guides our behavior, helps us make decisions, and tells us what is right and wrong. We display our values everyday by the way we speak and act. The decisions we make, the way we use our time, and how we spend our money all reveal our values.

"My son just doesn't have any values," complained an annoyed father. "Well," said his friend, "just what are your family's values?" "Ah, ummm, well, uhh," the first man stammered. "I guess I just haven't thought about it that way."

Often we haven't really thought about our values. We haven't thought about why people believe and act differently than we do. Discussing the differences in our beliefs can help us understand one another. Understanding our differences can promote a healthy tolerance for other people.

The rules we have in our families are a result of our values—the things we think are really important. It's vital that everyone know the difference between what's really important and what doesn't matter too much. Is not getting a haircut as important as not going to school? What can be negotiated and what is not negotiable?

In some families, everything is negotiable. In other families, nothing is negotiable. In still other families, what is negotiable and what isn't changes from day to day.

It is possible to be flexible and still be firmly based in solid values. The key is to decide what values are strictly not negotiable, as opposed to the things each family member can decide on their own. There are certain issues that require absolute obedience. President Abraham Lincoln said in his last public address, "Important principles may and must be inflexible." These inflexible rules need to be clearly defined and understood by all family members. On less important issues family members may choose for themselves. Many families quarrel about things that aren't on the "really important" list, and parents spend time being irritated unnecessarily. First parents, then families together, need to decide on important rules that must be obeyed and then "Don't sweat the small stuff."

Today people sometimes avoid declaring right from wrong. "After all," they say, "everyone has the right to their own ideas, and who is to say that parents should impose their thinking on their children?" Parents may argue that they don't want to require a lot of "do's" and don'ts." However, families who do not have a clear core of moral values deprive their children of a solid basis for approaching life. Children want and need boundaries. They need to be taught that in life there are principles of truth which, if lived, will bring happiness. If those principles, or moral values, are not a part of your life, the consequence is unhappiness. People in strong families are not afraid to talk about values. They don't crumble if everyone doesn't agree with their point of view. They know where they stand, and they're willing to be recognized for it.

Children from such families are able to move into society and do what they know is right, not just what others say they should. The more candid the discussion of values in the home, the better prepared family members are to act in harmony with their own standards. If decisions are made not just on the basis of what is easiest, cheapest, fastest, or what will "pay off," but what would be the right thing to do, children develop a higher sense of moral behavior. Such children would not have the same fuzzy thinking a college student did who explained that he had stolen a bike because "it wasn't locked." To this student his behavior was the fault of someone else. When people behave according to a set of clear standards, their sense of self-worth and self-respect is elevated. We define ourselves by our values.

Of course, the most important way to teach good moral values is by the example set in the home. Albert Schweitzer said, "There are three ways to teach a child. The first is by example. The second is by example. And the third is by example." Actions speak louder than words. What we do carries more weight than all the warnings and admonitions we can give.

Problem Prevention

Follow-up

(As a family discuss the assignment for the lesson Rules and Consequences.)

1. How do we feel about our family rules?
2. How about consequences to the rules? Did we decide on some consequences? Are we following through and applying consequences for disobedience? How are our attitudes?

Concept

To avoid conflicts, families should do all they can to prevent problems before they occur.

Rather than wait until a conflict arises, it is always better to anticipate it and avoid it.

There are several ways we can help prevent problems:

1. Use a kind tone of voice when speaking.
2. Communicate our feelings and let people know how they can help us.
3. Avoid sarcastic humor and eliminate criticism.

4. Try to sense how a family member is feeling and carefully speak or act in a way that will help him.
5. Keep an open mind and consider the ideas and suggestions of others. Don't be defensive.
6. Give one another high, positive expectations for behavior.

Example: Parent to child: "I know that as soon as you're finished eating, you'll start doing your homework."

Example: Child to parent: "I'm sure you'll try to understand what I have to say."

7. Think through and discuss possible problem situations before they happen.

Example: Ask, "What if a stranger asked to take you home?"

Example: Ask, "What if an older student pushed you at school?"

Talking about things that might occur helps us make decisions in advance. Hopefully, when the time comes to make a similar decision, we will have thought it through and will choose wisely. Preventing a problem is usually easier, and more desirable, than trying to solve the problem.

Family Survey Review

Statement #15. We try to prevent problems before they occur.

- When we see something that might become a problem, how do we try to prevent it?
- How can we improve in preventing family problems?

STORY

For years an old farmer plowed around a large rock in his field. The times he hit the rock by mistake resulted in one broken cultivator and two broken plowshares. Each time he approached the rock he worried about how much crop land he was losing because of it, and he resented the damage it had done to his equipment.

One day he decided he had suffered enough, and the farmer set out to dig the rock up and be done with it. Putting a large crowbar under one side, he found to his surprise that the rock was less than a foot deep in the ground. Soon he had it in his wagon and was carrying it away. The farmer smiled as he thought about how that "big" old rock had caused him many years of needless problems.

Discussion

1. How could the old farmer have prevented breaking his farm equipment?
2. Are we sometimes like the farmer? With just a little effort, can we avoid some of our problems? How can we do this?
3. How can talking with a caring person help prevent problems sometimes?

Activity

For our activity we're going to play the "What If?" game. We can use the questions in the lesson, or we can make up our own. Questions asked should be ones that can help us prevent possible problems. (*Everyone should participate in answering the questions.*)

1. What if a fire started in the home while you were alone?
2. What if you were at a party when people started doing things you think are wrong?
3. What if you were tending someone's child when he cut himself badly?
4. What if you were taking a test at school when the student behind you asked for an answer?
5. What if you were at a friend's house, and when it was time to go home, the movie you were watching wasn't finished?

Assignment

Choose one or both of the following assignments:

1. Read the Additional Solution for Success: Choices That Prevent and Solve Problems.
2. Read the Additional Solution for Success: Coping With Family Stress.

CHOICES THAT PREVENT AND SOLVE PROBLEMS

- **Simplify Your Life.** It's easy to get too busy. Whenever possible, eliminate activities that complicate your life. Choose the most important things and concentrate on them. Simplify your life.

- **Keep Things in Perspective.** Problems are a normal part of life. Remember that everyone has problems. Occasionally ask yourself, "Will this really matter in ten years?" Keep a long-term perspective on life and your problems.

- **Rid Yourself of Worries.** Worry weakens your energy. It reduces your ability to function well. Do something about the things that worry you. If you can't do anything about a problem, worrying won't make it better. When you wake up each morning, set goals you can reach that day. Do your best, then don't worry about things you can't do.

- **Live Outside of Yourself.** Helping others and providing support for others is a good way to forget your own problems. Develop friendships and positive relationships outside of your family. Love and care for people, animals and the environment. Living outside of yourself will bring you great joy.

- **Enjoy Nature as a Family.** Many families find outdoor activities refreshing. There is something special and rejuvenating about being out in nature. Try walks, picnics, camping, zoos, fishing, outdoor sports. Exercise is very beneficial to your well-being. Develop exercise habits you can enjoy as a family.

- **Develop a Sense of Humor.** Humor can drive away stress and worry. Humor can prevent problems in almost magical ways. Being able to laugh at some of the things that happen to us keeps life in perspective. Humor lightens loads and helps people relax. Laugh at yourself and laugh with others. Find the humor in your life.

COPING WITH FAMILY STRESS

We have heard much in recent years about how stress affects individuals. It can lead to health problems, emotional problems, and decreased productivity. How do families cope with stress?

Stress can cause some family members to get angry or depressed. However, members of healthy families have learned ways to cope with stress so they don't feel overwhelmed. A key to successfully dealing with stress is to develop an attitude of confidence in your ability to productively deal with life's challenges.

In their book, *Secrets of Strong Families,* family experts Nick Stinnet and John DeFrain have identified some coping skills which healthy families have in common. Not all families use every skill, but in their nationwide study of 3000 families they identified six keys to coping with stress successfully.

1. Seeing something good in the stress. Families who cope well are able to find something positive in the stress and crises they face. For example, a family in which the father became ill and unable to work was thankful that he was home more and could spend time with his children.

2. Pull together. Members of healthy families unite when problems occur. No individual feels as though he must face his problems alone. Family members support and help one another.

3. Call on others for help. In addition to relying on each other, members of healthy families turn to other resources for help. They seek out support from their church or synagogue, friends, neighbors, and their extended family. Family friends may help with childcare or meals during illness. A church group may take up a special collection. An important resource is the family's ability to talk about the problem with others.

4. Spiritual resources. Most families have spiritual convictions that help them cope with crises. Such convictions can be a source of stability to families who rely on them for a philosophy of life, perspective on the situation, and for hope and comfort.

5. Keep Communicating. Another resource that members of healthy families have is their ability to talk with each other during the crisis. For example, if one family member is struggling with grief or guilt over a mistake or a loss, the other family members are able to talk with him and help.

6. Go with the flow. Finally, strong families have learned that sometimes it is necessary to just stop fighting a problem and adapt to it. That may mean changing jobs, redefining who does what around the house, or cutting back on expenses. Even positive things like retirement, a wedding, or the birth of a child require the family to be adaptable and flexible. Being able to make necessary changes in family structure and how things are done enables families to solve problems and retain close relationships.

Successful families find a happy balance between stability and adaptability. For example, if Mom returns to work, some things, such as household chores, need to be adapted. Retaining other things, like bedtime stories or playing board games, can maintain stability.

We usually think of stress as something to be avoided. That is not possible, nor is it necessarily desirable. While stress that reaches unmanageable levels is destructive, some stress is good. It motivates us to do more, keeps life interesting, and it forces us to keep growing and learning.

A few additional thoughts on how to cope with stress:

- Keep things in perspective. Everybody has stress.
- Keep a sense of humor. Find something humorous in the situation.
- Take things one step, one day at a time.
- Stop worrying about things you can not control.
- Do not let little things diminish your happiness. Clear them up or forget them.
- Share your problems with others.
- If possible, change your routine. Get variety in your life.
- Take time for a favorite activity.
- Meditate; pray.
- Learn to relax and take a fresh look at the problem.
- Get outside.
- Exercise.
- Learn to say no; cut back on demands and commitments.

LESSON SIXTEEN

Problem Solving

Follow-up

(As a family discuss the assignment for the lesson Problem Prevention.)

1. What are some things we're doing to prevent problems in our family?
2. What more can we do to prevent possible problems?

Concept

Every family has problems. How we handle our problems makes all the difference. These are some ideas on how to solve problems:

1. Focus on the present, and be positive. Look toward a solution by asking, "How can we solve this problem?" instead of asking, "Why did this happen to us?" Try to see problems as challenges that you can overcome, and as possible opportunities to learn and grow.

2. Keep the channels of communication open. Expressing feelings is an important part of surviving a crisis. All family members need to know they are listened to and that their concerns are considered.

3. Seek solutions in small steps. Most problems don't have an "easy fix." Tackle problems one step at a time.

4. Draw on spiritual resources. God will sustain and strengthen families in time of need when families turn to him.

It will help families solve problems if they develop "We can do it together!" attitudes. Most problems can be solved when families talk about it as soon as the problem arises, discuss all possible solutions, then decide how they will "tackle it" together. Even huge conflicts can be resolved more easily when several people work together finding solutions.

Helping, supporting, and encouraging one another are keys to problem solving. Working through problems together strengthens relationships and helps bond family members to one another.

Family Survey Review

Statement # 16. We can talk about things without arguing.

- Why is it important to be able to talk about things without arguing?
- What are some things we can do to keep from arguing?

STORY

The Brooklyn Bridge that spans the river between Manhattan and Brooklyn is an engineering miracle. In 1883, a creative engineer, John Roebling, was inspired by an idea for this spectacular bridge project. However, bridge-building experts told him to forget it; it just was not possible. Roebling convinced his son, Washington, an up-and-coming engineer, that the bridge could be built. The two of them conceived the idea of how it could be accomplished and how to overcome the obstacles. Somehow they convinced bankers to finance the project. Then, with unharnessed excitement and energy, they hired their crew and began to build their dream bridge.

The project was only a few months under way when a tragic on-site accident killed John Roebling and severely injured his son. Washington was unable to talk or walk. Everyone thought the project would have to be scrapped, since the Roeblings were the only ones who understood how the bridge could be built.

Although Washington Roebling was unable to move or talk, his mind was sharp as ever. One day as he lay in his hospital bed, an idea flashed into his mind about how to develop a communication code. All he could move was one finger, so he touched the arm of his wife with that finger. He tapped out the code to communicate to her what to tell the engineers who continued building the bridge. For 13 long years, Washington tapped out his instructions with one finger until the spectacular Brooklyn Bridge was finally completed.

Discussion

1. Did Washington Roebling have a big problem?
2. Does every person and every family have problems?
3. What can we do as a family to improve our problem-solving skills?

Activity

First, let's talk about one problem that our family has. Let's decide today how we can work together to solve this problem.

Second, let's do the activity called Family Contracts.

Assignment

1. Make a greater effort to be aware of one another's problems.

Try to raise your level of sensitivity to better recognize the challenges in other people's lives.

2. Ask for help with problems when you need it.

Remember that to receive help with your problems, you need to share your concerns and challenges with those who care about you. There are always people who are willing to share your burdens.

3. Reach out to help others when they need you.

As a family, look around to those in need. You can help solve others' problems by giving of yourselves in service. Who is someone your family can help? What can you do to help them?

ACTIVITY
FAMILY CONTRACTS

Creativity can often solve conflicts between family members. Those involved must be willing to talk about the problem, decide what needs to be done about it, and agree to try new ways of acting towards one another. Sometimes it helps to "see" the problem and proposed solution by putting it into writing. Written contracts can help family members work together on agreeable solutions for everyone.

Activity

1. Family members with the problem choose a time to get together for a contract session.

2. Make sure everyone understands that the reason for getting together is not to argue or fight about the problem, but to think about ways to solve it.

3. Use the steps of negotiation briefly outlined here to discuss the problem and possible solutions.

   • Be specific about defining the problem and then brainstorm possible solutions.
   • Decide on a mutually agreeable solution.
   • Clearly define what each person agrees to do in order to make the solution work.
   • Discuss the consequences if either person fails to comply.

4. Put the agreement into writing by using the contract on the following page, or design your own.

ACTIVITY

SAMPLE CONTRACT

Use the following example as a guide when designing your own family contract. Encourage family members to be creative when putting their plan into words. Any format can be used as long as the contract is clear and understandable to everyone involved.

Whereas we,_____, and_____, hereby acknowledge that the following situation exists:
_____
_____
_____

therefore in order to constructively deal with the above, we do heretofore propose the following course of action:

We, _____, and _____, agree to_____.
In the event of non-compliance with the above terms: We agree to _____.
The following shall be an indication that the terms of this contract have been successfully completed _____
And in this event, we do solemnly agree to the following reward:_____

Date: _____

Signed:_____

Signed:_____

CHOICES

A Lesson Learned

I walked with my friend, a Quaker, to the newsstand the other night, and he bought a paper, thanking the newsie politely. The newsie didn't even acknowledge it.

"A sullen fellow, isn't he?" I commented.

"Oh, he's that way every night," shrugged my friend.

"Then why do you continue to be so polite to him?" I asked.

"Why not?" inquired my friend. "Why should I let him decide how I'm going to act?"

As I thought about this incident later, it occurred to me that the important word was "act." My friend acts toward people; most of us react toward them. He has a sense of inner balance which is lacking in most of us; he knows who he is, what he stands for, how he should behave. He refuses to return incivility for incivility, because then he would not be in command of his own conduct.

Nobody is unhappier than the perpetual reactor. His center of emotional gravity is not rooted within himself, where it belongs, but in the world outside him. His temperature is always being raised or lowered by the social climate around him, and he is a mere creature at the mercy of these elements.

Serenity cannot be achieved until we become the masters of our own actions and attitudes. To let another person determine whether we shall be rude or gracious, elated or depressed, is to relinquish control over our own personalities, which is ultimately all we possess. The only true possession is self-possession.

— Sydney J. Harris

Obedience

More than a century ago, nobility of England, in their colorful finery, were on a fox hunt. They came to a closed gate, where nearby sat a ragged youngster.

"Open the gate, lad," said the leader of the hunt.

"No, this property belongs to my father, and he desires it left shut."

"Open the gate, lad. Do you know who I am?"

"No, sir."

"I am the Duke of Wellington."

"The Duke of Wellington, this nation's hero, would not ask me to disobey my father."

And the riders of the hunt silently rode on.

— Author Unknown

If

If you can keep your head when all about you

Are losing theirs and blaming it on you;

If you can trust yourself when all men doubt you,

But make an allowance for their doubting too;

If you can wait and not be tired by waiting,

Or, being lied about, don't deal in lies,

Or being hated, don't give way to hating,

And yet don't look too good, nor talk too wise;

If you can dream—and not make dreams your master;

If you can think—and not make thoughts your aim;

If you can meet with triumph and disaster

And treat those two imposters just the same;

If you can bear to hear the truth you've spoken

Twisted by knaves to make a trap for fools,

Or watch the things you gave your life to, broken,

And stoop and build 'em up with worn out tools;

If you can make one heap of all your winnings

And risk it on one turn of pitch-and-toss,

And lose, and start again at your beginnings

And never breathe a word about your loss;

If you can force your heart and nerve and sinew
To serve your turn long after they are gone,
And so hold on when there is nothing in you
Except the will which says to them: "Hold on!"

If you can talk with crowds and keep your virtue,
Or walk with kings—nor lose the common touch;
If neither foes nor loving friends can hurt you;
If all men count with you, but none too much;
If you can fill the unforgiving minute
With sixty seconds worth of distance run—
Yours is the Earth and everything that's in it,
And—which is more—you'll be a Man, my son!

— Richard Kipling

One Heart

If I can stop one heart from breaking.
I shall not live in vain;
If I can ease one life the aching,
Or cool one pain,
Or help one fainting robin
Unto his nest again,
I shall not live in vain.

— Emily Dickinson

Around the Corner

Around the corner I have a friend,
In this great city that has no end;
Yet days go by, and weeks rush on,
And before I know it a year is gone,
And I never see my old friend's face,
For life is a swift and terrible race.
He knows I like him just as well
As in the days when I rang his bell
And he rang mine. We were younger then.

And now we are busy, tired men:
Tired with playing a foolish game,
Tired with trying to make a name.
"Tomorrow," I say, "I will call on Jim,
Just to show that I'm thinking of him."
But tomorrow comes—and tomorrow goes
And the distance between us grows and grows.
Around the corner! Yet miles away…
"Here's a telegram, sir."
Jim died today.
And that's what we get, and deserve in the end:
Around the corner, a vanished friend.

— Charles Hanson Towne

Why Not?

You see things; and you say
"Why?"
But I dream things that never were;
And I say "why not?"

— George Bernard Shaw

Positive Attitude

If you think you are beaten, you are.
If you think you dare not, you don't.
If you'd like to win but think you can't,
It's almost a cinch you won't.
Life's battles don't always go
To the stronger or faster man.
But soon or late the man who wins
Is the man who thinks he can.

— Author Unknown

Choices

You are the person who has to decide
Whether you'll do it or toss it aside;
You are the person who makes up your mind
Whether you'll lead or will linger behind
Whether you'll try for the goal that is afar
Or just be contented to stay where you are.
What do you wish? To be known as a shirk,
Known as a good man who's willing to work,
Scorned as a loafer, or praised by your chief
Rich man or poor man or beggar or thief?
Eager or earnest or dull through the day?
Honest or crooked? It's you who must say!
You must decide in the face of the test
Whether you'll shirk or give it your best.
Nobody here will compel you to rise;
No one will force you to open your eyes;
No one will answer for you yes or no,
Whether to stay or whether you go;
Life is a game, but it's you who must say
Whether as cheat or as sportsman you'll play.
Fate may betray you, but you settle first
Whether to live to your best or your worst.
So whatever it is you are wanting to be
Remember, to fashion the choice you are free,
Kindly or selfish, or gentle or strong,
Keeping the right way or taking the wrong
Careless of honor or guarding your pride
All these are questions which you must decide.
Yours the selection, whichever you do;
The thing men call character is all up to you.

— Author Unknown

CHAPTER FIVE

Well-Being

SOLUTION

INTRODUCTION FOR PARENTS

A businessman shared what he learned about well-being when he told this story:

"I started my adult life with a bang, you might say. My parents were moderately well-to-do and gave me a good start in my own business. It flourished and things looked rosy for ten years or so. Then the economy went sour at about the time I had made some risky investments. One by one those went down the tubes. In the end we lost everything—house, cars and the business.

My wife and I sat out by the lake one night and talked until the sun came up. I remember feeling like I had been stripped of everything—like I had been robbed. 'Why try again? I asked her. 'We may work and work only to lose it.' We struggled with that a long time. Finally, we decided that we had been thinking wrong. The purpose of life isn't to accumulate money, swimming pools, cars and fur coats. The purpose of life is to enjoy life because it is a precious gift— to cherish your family and friends, to become a better person intellectually and spiritually and to help other people. The investments of time and effort I make in family and friends, in charitable work and in improving myself can never be lost. Things in the mind and heart cannot be taken away.

We did start over again and have enjoyed success. We've replaced many of the material things we lost, but most importantly, we have changed our thoughts. The job, the possessions, the money are no longer an end in themselves. They are a means of making life pleasant and serving others. If I lost them all tomorrow, I would still feel rich."

Total well-being is an ideal state when a balance is achieved in the six areas of life: physical, mental, social, emotional, financial and spiritual. Realistically, however, seldom do individuals or families enjoy well-being in every area at the same time. For example, even though we may enjoy total physical well-being, if we are stressed financially, we don't have peace of mind. The reverse can also be true. If we have financial independence, but we are burdened with serious ill-health, we don't enjoy total well-being. Achieving a balance in all areas is a process and a goal.

The wisest course individuals and families can follow is to make the kind of choices that will insure well-being in as many areas as possible.

Families who enjoy well-being:

    1. Demonstrate love and respect for one another. Where love is, harmony exists. Parents and children make sincere efforts to unselfishly maintain peace in the home.

    2. Have a positive outlook on life. Positive attitudes are contagious. In families we have incredible power to affect one another with our attitudes—in positive and negative ways. A saying that I heard once was posted on our refrigerator for years: "Be wise if you can, be pretty if you are, but be cheerful if it kills you!" Optimism and a sense of humor are virtues every family needs in large quantities.

    3. Help one another live the values they believe, and reach the goals they set. There truly is strength in numbers. When we, in our families, openly discuss our values, and together set rules and goals, there is strength. We can feel the unity and power of our family, and it's a good feeling.

    4. Work toward reaching their individual potentials within a caring, supportive environment. What a difference it makes when our family supports us in our interests and activities! We're usually happier and more successful when our family is "there for us" when we need them.

    5. Build strong relationships with one another. People aren't best friends just because they were born into the same family. Strong relationships require time and effort. Usually good relationships result from years of speaking and acting in ways that demonstrate concern and affection. Family members have countless opportunities to build strong, long-lasting relationships. That's one of the blessings of being a family.

    6. Live a healthy lifestyle. When we're free from illness and pain we can more easily work on reaching our mental, social, emotional, financial and spiritual goals. Health is a gift we should work daily to protect.

    7. Encourage the mental development of each family member. Strong families help one another with school and work assignments, read books, share uplifting music, and encourage all intellectual growth.

    8. Promote and teach social skills. Through example and precept parents can teach many of the social skills that will benefit their children throughout their lives.

> **Benefits of Being a "Well" Family**
>
> - Family members feel loved and accepted.
> - Feelings of well-being help family members want to spend time together.
> - The well-being of family members helps open the channels of communication.
> - The ability to deal with crisis is improved.
> - Well-being helps support family commitment.

9. Attain an emotional balance. Families who enjoy well-being discuss problems before they get out of control. They have learned that extreme reactions are not productive.

10. Achieve financial stability. Healthy families recognize the difference between a "need" and a "want." They live in such a way that money doesn't become a source of conflict.

11. Cultivate a level of spirituality. Many strong families have a belief in a Supreme Being which strengthens and sustains them.

12. Recognize problems and conflicts, but focus on their ability to deal with the problems and grow from the challenges. With most family problems the entire family should gather together, discuss the problem, and consider possible solutions. After every family member has shared his or her opinion, a solution is chosen and the family works together to solve the problem. During family discussions and after problems are past the crisis stage, ask questions like, "How can we learn from this?" or "What can we do to prevent this from happening again?" Strong families learn and grow closer from their challenges.

It is apparent that there are serious problems in this world. Many people stand in need of help. However, it is also true that there is much happiness and well-being in the world. When individuals enjoy well-being and are members of strong families, those individuals can encourage well-being in others, and can contribute to the success of communities and nations.

Just as we grow and develop one day at a time as individuals, as a family well-being is a process. Creating things of worth usually takes time and much effort. We need to be kind and patient with ourselves, and with our families, as we strive to achieve well-being.

LESSON SEVENTEEN

Physical Well-Being

Follow-up

(As a family discuss the assignment for the lesson Problem Solving.)

1. What did we learn from the lesson on problem-solving?
2. How have we improved our problem-solving skills?

Concept

Keeping our bodies healthy is important. People usually can be more effective in other areas of their lives (mental, social, temporal) if their bodies are healthy. Families who have a healthy lifestyle try to:

1. Drink plenty of clean water.
2. Eat well-balanced meals, including fruits, vegetables and whole grains.
3. Exercise regularly.
4. Get adequate sleep.
5. Avoid harmful drugs, tobacco and excessive alcohol.

Being healthy affects the quality of our lives. Having a healthy body gives us the energy and ability to do our daily activities, and our outlook on life is usually better. When our physical needs have been met, we can better reach out to meet the needs of others.

Family Survey Review

Statement # 17. Our family has good health habits.

- Why is it important to keep ourselves healthy and physically fit?
- How are we doing with our health habits?
- Do we eat healthfully? Do we exercise regularly?
- How can we improve?

STORY

Thousands of years ago, a slave named Aesop wrote some simple fables (stories) that show common principles of thought and behavior. One such fable is that of the deer and the hunter. The deer was admiring his reflection in the pool.

"Ah," said he, "where can you see such noble horns as these, with such antlers? I wish I had legs worthy to bear such a glorious crown. It is a pity they are so slim and unsightly." At that moment, a hunter appeared and sent an arrow flying towards the deer. The deer bounded off, and by means of his nimble legs, about which he was just complaining, was quickly out of range of the hunter.

Prize yourself. Be grateful for the body you have, and appreciate your unique talents and strengths. Build on those strengths; don't tear yourself down or focus on your weaknesses. Instead, think and act in ways that will make you like yourself. Don't compare yourself to other people, and don't compare what you are now to what you think you should be. Celebrate who you are, and be the best you can be. If you're doing your very best to reach the goals you've set for yourself, you're doing enough.

Discussion

1. Are we sometimes like the deer in the story? Are we unhappy with some part of our physical body?
2. What do we think and say that shows we compare ourselves with others?
3. How can we build on our strengths and not dwell on our weaknesses?

Activity

Improve your physical well-being by doing something active as a family. Go on a walk, swim, play ball or anything you choose. This activity should include everyone.

Ask: "Can we go on a family walk right now?" If not now, ask, "When can we do something active as a family?"

Assignment

The assignment is to make a specific plan of how your family will improve its physical well-being. Then the challenge is to do it. On the following page there is a list of Solution Suggestions to use as a resource of ideas.

PHYSICAL WELL-BEING

1. Go on a walk

2. Ride a bike.

3. Swim.

4. Go hiking.

5. Exercise while you watch TV.

6. Play tag.

7. Lift weights.

9. Play Frisbee in the park.

10. Play ball—soccer, kickball, basketball, softball.

Mental Well-Being

Follow-up

(As a family discuss the assignment for the lesson Physical Well-Being.)

1. What improvements have we made in our eating and exercising habits?
2. Did we make a plan of how we'll improve our physical well-being? If not, let's stop and decide on some ways we can do this. *(Ideas are in the Physical Well-being Lesson.)*

If we have a plan for improvement, what are we doing to follow it?

Concept

A person with good mental well-being has an optimistic outlook on life, enjoys learning, and is interested in improving his mind. He wants to know about many subjects, and he welcomes new information that will help him understand himself, other people, and the world.

One ideal way to improve our minds is to read. Through books we are taught important lessons from history; we can visit any place in the world, and become experts on countless subjects.

One good place to learn is at the dinner table. When families are all together they can talk about what they learned that day. Parents can tell about interesting things that happened at work, or discuss local and national news. Children can share the events of their day at school and play.

Instead of watching television, families can choose to enjoy activities that will improve their lives and strengthen their relationships. A list of "Things To Do Instead Of Watching TV" is included in this lesson.

The well-known artist known as Whistler had ideas about how we can enjoy mental well-being. Whistler said, "Hang on the walls of your mind the memory of your successes. Take counsel of your strength, not your weakness. Think of the good jobs you have done. Think of the times when you rose above your average level of performance and carried out an idea or a dream or a desire for which you had deeply longed. Hang these pictures on the walls of your mind and look at them as you travel the roadway of life."

We will be contributing to our mental well-being when we think good thoughts about ourselves, our circumstances, our family, our neighbors and all we meet. Happiness is not a destination, it is a state of mind. President Abraham Lincoln said, "Most folks are about as happy as they make up their minds to be."

Family Survey Review

Statement #18. We enjoy learning in our family.

- What are some of the ways people learn that our family would enjoy?
- How do you feel about sharing at the dinner table one thing you learned each day?

STORY

A man was complaining to a friend about his trials and difficulties. After a while the complaining became too much for the friend. "I see you have been living on Grumbling Street. I lived there myself for some time and never enjoyed good health. The air was bad, the house bad, the water bad; the birds never came and sang in the streets, and I was quite gloomy and sad. But I moved. I found myself a house on Thanksgiving Street, and ever since, I have had good health, and so has my family. The air is pure, the water pure, the house good. The sun shines on it all day, and I am as happy as I can be. Now I recommend that you move, too. There are plenty of houses available on Thanksgiving Street, and I'm sure you'd find yourself to be a new man. I would be glad to have you as a neighbor!"

Discussion

1. What does it mean to live on Grumbling Street?
2. Has our family ever lived on Grumbling Street? When?
3. What does it mean to live on Thanksgiving Street? Shall we move there? When?

Activity

For the activity, parents are to lead the following discussion:

Often television programs teach children things they shouldn't learn. Parents wouldn't think of letting someone come into their home and teach children to be disrespectful to adults, exhibit low moral values, and enjoy violence. Yet that is what's happening when children are allowed to watch excessive, unmonitored TV. Educational and uplifting programs are available, and families can share special times watching together. Television can be used as a tool for learning good things. However, families need to have a plan for television watching.

Let's talk about our family's habits of television viewing. Do we have a problem? How do we all feel about the number of hours spent watching TV in our home? Below is a list of things to do instead of watching TV. If our family has a problem with too much television viewing, let's decide on some limits. Then let's choose activities from the list below to do instead of watching TV. Let's schedule the activities and do them.

Breaking bad habits is difficult, but not impossible. It will bring rewards of closer family relationships and increased mental well-being.

Look at the list below and participate in some activities together.

Things To Do Instead of Watching TV

- Do a kind deed for someone.
- Do your homework.
- Practice a musical instrument.
- Help with the housework or the yard work.
- Work on a hobby or begin a new hobby.
- Visit someone who is sick or shut in.
- Read.
- Exercise.
- Write a letter.
- Play a sport.
- Invite a friend to visit.
- Finish an unfinished project.
- Cook.

- Play a board or card game.
- Listen to music.
- Go to a movie, play or concert.
- Put together a puzzle.
- Go on a hike or picnic.
- Do your homework.
- Go swimming.

Assignment

The assignment for this lesson is to do one of the things listed below to increase your mental well-being:

1. Take a trip to the library.
2. Enjoy an evening reading as a family with the television off.
3. Assign family members to bring one item of educational interest or information about a current event to discuss at the dinner table.
4. Give a lesson that teaches a moral value.
5. As a family discuss what to do in case of a fire or other emergency.

If time and interest allow, do the activity on the following page: Family Yearbook and/or read the Additional Solution For Success: Family Esteem.

ACTIVITY
FAMILY YEARBOOK

Now and then it's enjoyable to reflect on important, often life-changing family events of the past. This activity can help you look back and recall past times, discuss the important things that have happened in your family, and renew a long-term perspective and appreciation for one another.

Activity

1. At the end of the year, gather together all the photos taken of your family that year.
2. Choose the photos that best show favorite past events.
3. Decide how to organize the photos. You may want to use them

   - in the order they were taken
   - in sections for each member
   - in sections according to themes (trips, school, etc.)

4. Secure the pictures in a safe, archival format and write captions.
5. Include other mementos, such as postcards, invitations, or announcements, if you like.
6. Have pages at the back of your yearbook for everyone to write their name and comments about the year.

ADDITIONAL SOLUTION FOR SUCCESS
FAMILY ESTEEM

Just as individuals need to feel good about themselves in order to be successful, families need to have a feeling of worth and value about themselves as a group. They need to be able to look to the future with confidence that they can be successful.

Families can learn to believe in themselves and their ability to solve problems and be happy. This belief begins with an understanding that each family is unique with its own special talents and strengths.

In all the world there isn't another family exactly like yours. There isn't any other family made up of exactly the same people, with the same combination of talents, skills, challenges, etc. No other family has had just the same experiences, felt the same joys, or experienced quite the same disappointments. Your family has its own terms for certain things, private nicknames for each other, and your own stories and jokes. Of all the families that have ever been formed, or will be formed in the future, there has never been, or ever will be, another one exactly like yours.

In addition to appreciating their worth together, strong families value each individual family member. They know that each person contributes something to the family that no one else can. The family's belief in each one of its members creates a great sense of self-worth and security for each individual. In turn, the self-esteem of each individual contributes to the whole family's sense of worth.

For those who value their family, how they see themselves is more important than what others think of them. Believing in and accepting who we are is one of the most difficult challenges in life. We are constantly bombarded with messages like "What makes you think you can do it?" "Kids your size can't be on the team." "You're too fat to be a cheerleader." "Why doesn't your family get a decent car?" We must have a personal awareness of our worth regardless of how other people judge us. If we can believe in ourselves, the self-defeating messages from all sides of who we ought to be, or what we ought to be like, cannot damage our sense of worth.

When the great scientist Albert Einstein was ten years old, he was told by his school teacher, "You will never amount to much." Einstein later wrote, "Try not to become a man of 'success' but rather a man of value." He was able to be himself, ignoring the false opinion of others. Like many other successful people, Einstein believed that no one can make you feel inferior without your consent. In other words, what other people think of us isn't important unless we let it be. When family members are determined to believe in themselves, it is easier for each family member to believe in himself, too.

The poet e. e. cummings recognized the same challenges when he wrote, "To be nobody but yourself, in a world which is doing its best, night and day, to make you everybody else, is to fight the hardest battle there is. Never stop fighting."

In reality, to base our sense of worth on what others think of us is to be more responsible to them than we are to ourselves. Let's not allow our family's esteem be determined by outside influences.

Social Well-Being

Follow-up

(As a family discuss the assignment for the lesson Mental Well-Being.)

1. What are some of the things we've learned which improve our mental well-being?
2. Are our dinner conversations more enjoyable? If not, what can we do to improve?

Concept

One of the roads to happiness is social well-being. When we are socially involved with others, we're usually happier and feel a part of a larger group. Supportive friends, extended family, and our neighbors can give us help and encouragement when needed. We all like to know that people care about us.

Also, families are happier when they reach out in acts of kindness and service to meet the needs of others. Albert Pipe wrote, "What we have done for ourselves alone dies with us. What we have done for others and the world remains and is immortal."

What is social well-being? It is:

• feeling accepted in a group.
• helping others feel appreciated and accepted.
• spending quality time with others.
• communicating openly and listening well.
• helping people deal with conflict and crises in constructive ways.
• committing time and energy to causes that benefit others.

A song called "No Man Is An Island" tells how man doesn't go through life alone. We are dependent on one another for our happiness and well-being. A few of the words are:

No man is an island
No man stands alone
Each man's joy is joy to me
Each man's grief is my own

To enjoy social well-being in our families we need to interact with other people, be involved with those who can help and strengthen us when needed, and reach beyond our own concerns to be part of a support system for others. As we share our lives we'll experience the joys of social well-being.

Family Survey Review

Statement # 19. Our family enjoys being with other people.

• How can our family be more friendly and social?
• What can we do to be of service to our extended family and to our friends?

STORY

Sam Foss liked to walk. He had wandered a little too far in the blazing sun, while lost in his thoughts, and now suddenly he realized how hot and tired he was. The big tree at the side of the road looked tempting, and he stopped for a moment to rest in its shade.

There was a little sign on the tree, which he read with surprise and pleasure. "There is a good spring inside the fence. Come and drink if you are thirsty."

Foss climbed over the fence, found the spring, and gratefully drank his fill of the cool water. Then he noticed a bench near the spring on which was tacked another sign. He went over to it and read, "Sit down and rest awhile if you are tired."

Now thoroughly delighted, he went to a barrel of apples nearby, and saw that here, too, was a sign. "If you like apples, just help yourself," he read. He accepted the invitation, picked out a plump red apple and looked up to discover an elderly man watching him with interest.

"Hello, there!" he called. "Is this your place?"

"Yes," the old man answered. "I'm glad you stopped by." He explained the reason for the signs. The water was going to waste; the bench was gathering dust in the attic; the apples were more than he could use. He and his wife thought it would be neighborly to offer tired, thirsty passers-by a place to rest and refresh themselves. So they had brought down the bench and put up the signs, and thereby made themselves a host of fine new friends.

"You must like people," Foss said.

"Of course!" the old man answered simply. "Don't you?"

Discussion

1. Did the sharing man help make other people happy?
2. Can we share something we have to make another family happy? What?
3. Is life more enjoyable with friends? How can we be better friends?

Activity

The activity for this lesson is to do something as a family that will improve our social well-being. Here are some ideas:

1. Meet all of our neighbors.
2. Volunteer our time in service to the community.
3. Visit a nursing home or hospital.
4. Invite friends to dinner, or to play games with our family.
5. Do something kind for a neighbor.
6. Call a friend or relative we haven't spoken to for a long time.

Assignment

The assignment is to make a specific plan of how your family will improve its social well-being. Then the challenge is to do it.

FAMILY FUN

Most families agree that it's important to spend "quality" time together. But the realities of busy lives often prevent family members from enjoying family fun. This activity is designed to help us make definite plans that include our entire family, and to turn those plans into reality.

1. Let's take a sheet of paper and fold it in half. On one side, we'll write our ideas for things our family can do together at no cost (playing games, taking a hike, etc.) On the other side, we'll write ideas for things our family can do that cost money. (movies, dinner in a restaurant, vacations, etc.)

2. Now let's read all of the ideas and cross out activities that we're not really interested in.

3. Let's talk about all of the activities that don't cost money. Next, we'll copy the good suggestions onto small slips of paper, put them into a jar or box, and label it "FREE FUN."

4. Let's discuss the ideas that do cost money. We'll put the list of activities that cost money into a jar or box we label "FUN FUNDS." Now let's decide how our family can save money to put in the box. Here are some ideas to consider:

- Everyone agrees to "pledge" an amount from paychecks or allowances each week.
- Everyone agrees to give 10% of all gift money received for birthdays, holidays and special occasions.
- At the end of each day, everyone tosses in all of their loose change.
- All loose change left in pockets from the laundry goes in the box.
- Family members can donate the money received from recycling aluminum cans, or another fund-raising project.
- Parents might agree to "match" whatever amount has been saved during a time period.

5. Let's schedule at least one time each week for our family to do something together from the "FREE FUN" box.

6. Now we need to decide what our family wants to do first from the "FUN FUNDS" box. As soon as there is enough money, we'll schedule a time for the activity and start saving for the next one on the list.

7. When our family has used all the ideas in the boxes, we can start over again.

BEING PART OF AN EXTENDED FAMILY

A sense of belonging and increased social well-being comes from being part of an extended family. This includes feeling a part of our family's history and knowing the stories about our Grandpa and Grandma, and the way life was for our ancestors. It also involves feeling an interest and concern for the younger members of the extended family.

People with a strong sense of family pass on the stories of deceased family members so that younger members can learn about their roots. Alex Haley, author of the book *Roots,* tells about the outpouring of interest American families had in the history he uncovered regarding African-Americans. Mr. Haley believes that many people feel a little empty because they don't know about their ancestors. Preserving and passing on family history is important for a family's sense of continuity. The feeling a family have about who they are, because of an ancestor's example, or learning about how ancestors coped with adversities, can be a source of strength. Looking at our ancestors' lives and history can also help us put our problems in perspective. The struggles they endured and the joys they felt give us a better understanding of ourselves.

In addition to learning from their family history, families can also learn much from their living relatives. Grandparents and other relatives who give their time and love to children strengthen them. Relatives can tell the children what their parents were like as children. From their experience, they can teach and share valuable advice. Quite often grandparents are the nucleus of extended family activities.

An appreciation for the past also demonstrates to older relatives a respect for their values and accomplishments. The life of grandparents can be given renewed meaning by a grandchild's interest in their past.

Strong families keep in touch with their extended family. They pass news back and forth, they exchange pictures, or they call each other for no particular reason. Families who live far apart may do things such as circulate a letter to which each family adds his or her own news before mailing it on. They may make tape-recordings for family members far away. Some families devote a whole wall to pictures of grandparents, aunts, uncles and cousins. The key is having enough contact with each other so that relatives feel like relatives, not strangers.

To strengthen your family's ties to your extended family, conduct a little quiz about your relatives. Add as many questions as you would like.

For children:

- Who is our oldest relative?
- Who is our youngest relative?
- How many cousins do we have?
- How are we related to all our aunts and uncles?
- Where did our ancestors come from? Where did they live? What were their names? What did they do?
- Where were our grandparents (or some other relative) born?
- How old are they?
- What did they do for a living?

For parents:

- What do you remember most about your grandparents?
- As a little child?
- As a teenager?
- As an adult?
- What other relative was a favorite of yours? Why?
- What things did you do with relatives when you were growing up?

For everyone:

- What is the importance of our extended family?
- What things do we not know about our family's history that we would like to know?
- Are there relatives with whom we would like to spend more time?
- What can we do to strengthen our extended family relationships?

LESSON TWENTY

Financial Well-Being

Follow-up

(As a family discuss the assignment for the lesson Social Well-Being.)

1. What are we doing to know our neighbors and extended family members better?
2. What acts of kindness and service have we performed since our last lesson?

Concept

Ideally, families should live in such a way that money doesn't become a source of conflict. Usually our financial problems aren't money problems, they're attitude and behavior problems.

What are some things we can do to meet our basic needs and reach our financial goals?

We can:

- **Learn.** Do our best to get a good education, and continue learning.
- **Work diligently.** There is no substitute for simply working hard to get what we want in life.

- **Job development.** Continue looking for educational and job opportunities that will qualify us for better employment or improve our life.
- **Plan.** Make a plan for how we'll spend our income.
- **Commit.** Commit to our plan of how we'll spend our income. For example, we must realize that there will be times when we have to wait for something we want until there is money for it. Sometimes we can live without things we "want" but don't really "need."
- **Live the plan.** There will sometimes be unexpected bills, but as a rule, we should live by a plan that will keep us as debt-free as possible. If we really want to be out of debt we should decide that there will be no more charging or borrowing money. Nothing will be purchased until there is enough money to pay for it.
- **Save for the future.** We should try to save some of our money each month for our future needs and for unexpected bills.

When families make wise financial decisions and live within their means, they experience less stress and fewer problems, and they can enjoy financial well-being.

Family Survey Review

Statement #20. Our family makes wise financial decisions.

- What good decisions do we make with our money?
- How can we stay out of debt?
- What should we do to save money?

STORY

An old fable tells about an ant and a grasshopper. All summer long the ant busily worked, preparing for the cold winter ahead. The grasshopper watched the ant and laughed at her. "Stop working and come and play!" the grasshopper said. "Don't worry about winter. The sun is shining and we are young!" Nevertheless, the ant continued to put away food, preparing for the months ahead. The grasshopper kept playing. Before too long, the snow fell and their world became a white, frozen land. The ant was snug and warm, with plenty of food in her little home. The grasshopper, you might guess, was miserably cold and hungry.

Discussion

    1. What can we learn from the ant?
    2. What do we learn from the grasshopper?
    3. Is our family like the ant or the grasshopper? How?

Activity

Running our home costs money. We need a budget to help us stay out of debt. It's easier to live debt-free when we understand how much money we have to work with, and what our family expenses are. This activity can help us look at our monthly expenses and see where the money is spent. First, let's guess the answers to these questions:

    1. What is the price of a gallon of milk?
    2. What is the price of a loaf of bread?
    3. What does our family spend each month on food?
    4. How much does it cost to fill the car with gas?
    5. What do we pay each month for rent (or the mortgage payment)?
    6. What was last month's telephone bill?
    7. How much did we pay last month for gas and electricity?
    8. How much does it cost to have the dentist fill a cavity?
    9. What does it cost to replace a light bulb?
  10. How much does it cost to go to college?

Let's play the MONEY GAME. In preparation for this game, a parent will need to have real or pretend money in the amount of your monthly paycheck or the amount you use for paying bills. On the table, display all the money. Ask: "Family, how much of this money does it take to pay the rent (mortgage) for one month?" Take that amount away and put it in an envelope.

Ask: "How much money does it take to buy the food for one month?" Put that amount in an envelope.

Ask: "How much money does it take to pay the utilities bill?" Put that amount in an envelope.

Do this until all of your bills are "paid."

Ask: "Family, how much money does our family have left each month for extra purchases? How much money do we have to save? What should we do about this?"

Assignment

1. Decide as a family on a budget. First, list all of your bills and expenses. Decide how much money you have to spend on your "needs." Now talk about your "wants" and how much money you should spend on those. Last, discuss how much money your family should save each month and how you will do that.

2. For one week, each family member should keep a record of every purchase. Then meet again and discuss how well you're staying within your budget.

3. Each day try to make choices that will help you be debt-free and save for the future.

4. Read the Ten Financial Principles on the following page.

TEN FINANCIAL PRINCIPLES

Principle 1: Financial problems are usually behavioral problems rather than money problems.

Principle 2: If you continue doing what you have been doing, you'll continue getting what you have been getting.

Principle 3: Nothing (no thing) is worth risking the loss of a relationship.

Principle 4: Money spent on things you value usually leads to a feeling of satisfaction and accomplishment. Money spent on things you don't value usually leads to a feeling of frustration and futility.

Principle 5: We know the price of everything and the value of nothing.

Principle 6: You can never get enough of what you don't need, because what you don't need can never satisfy you.

Principle 7: Financial freedom is more often the result of decreased spending than of increased income.

Principle 8: Be grateful for what you have.

Principle 9: The best things in life are free.

Principle 10: The value of an individual should never be equated with the worth of an individual.

SOLUTIONS THROUGH STORIES AND POEMS

WELL-BEING

The Little Parable for Mothers

The young mother set her foot on the path of life. "Is the way long?" she asked. And her guide said, "Yes. And the way is hard. And you will be old before you reach the end of it. But the end will be better than the beginning."

But the young mother was happy, and would not believe that anything could be better than these years. So she played with her children and gathered flowers for them along the way and bathed them in clear streams, and the sun shone on them, and life was good, and the mother cried, "Nothing will ever be lovelier than this."

Then came night, and storm, and the path was dark, and the children shook with fear and cold, and the mother drew them close and covered them with her mantle, and the children said, "Oh, Mother, we are not afraid for you are near and no harm can come." And the mother said, "This is better than the brightness of day, for I have taught my children courage. Today, I have given them strength."

And the next day came strange clouds which darkened the earth–clouds of war and hate and evil, and the children groped and stumbled, and the mother said, "Look up. Life your eyes to the light." And the children looked and saw above the clouds an Everlasting Glory, and it guided them and brought them beyond the darkness. And that night, the mother said, "This is the best day of all, for I have shown my children God."

And the days went on, and the weeks, and months and the years, and the mother grew old, and she was little and bent. But her children were tall and strong and walked with courage. And when the way was hard, they helped their mother, and when the way was rough, they lifted her, for she was as light as a feather, and at last they came to a hill, and beyond this hill they could see a shining road and golden gates flung wide.

And mother said, "I have reached the end of my journey. And now I know that the end is better than the beginning, for my children can walk alone, and their children after them."

The children said, "You will always walk with us, Mother, even when you have gone through the gates."

And they stood and watched her as she went on alone, and the gates closed after her. And they said, "We cannot see her, but she is with us still. A mother like ours is more than a memory. She is a Living Presence."

— Temple Bailey

Living From Within

The story is told of a philosopher who stood at the gate of an ancient city greeting travelers who wished to enter. One of them questioned him:

"What kind of people live in your city?"

The philosopher met the question with a counter question: "What kind of people lived in the city from whence you came?"

"Oh, they were very bad people," answered the traveler, "cruel, deceitful, and devil-worshiping."

"That's the kind of people who live in this city," declared the philosopher.

Another traveler came by and asked the same question, to which the philosopher replied: "What kind of people lived in the city from whence you came?"

"Oh, they were good people," answered the second traveler, "kind, and truthful, and God-loving."

"That's the kind of people who live in this city," declared the philosopher.

— Dr. David Goodman

Your Mind's Garden

What seed have you sown in your garden of mind?

What thoughts have you sent into space?

Remember they yield you a harvest in kind

A life you henceforth must face.

For you are the sower, you choose your own seed
You fashion your future each day
Your garden is fertile, producing with speed
The fruit of each thought tucked away.

So if you wish happiness, health and peace
Then choose well each seed as you sow
Your future is shaped by the thoughts you release
Each hour, each day as you go.

— Elizabeth B. Waddell

Twelve Guideposts for Living

I will do more than belong—I will participate.
I will do more than care—I will help.
I will do more than believe—I will practice.
I will do more than be fair—I will be kind.
I will do more than forgive—I will forget.
I will do more than dream—I will work.
I will do more than teach—I will inspire.
I will do more than earn—I will enrich.
I will do more than give—I will serve.
I will do more than live—I will grow.
I will do more than be friendly—I will be a friend.
I will do more than be a citizen—I will be a patriot.

— Author Unknown

There are nine requisites for contented living: health enough to make work a pleasure; wealth enough to support your needs; strength enough to battle with difficulties and overcome them; grace enough to confess your sins and forsake them; patience enough to toil until some good is accomplished; charity enough to see some good in your neighbors; love enough to move you to be useful and helpful to others; faith enough to make real the things of God; hope enough to remove all anxious fears concerning the future.

— Goethe

A Recipe for Home

One-half cup friendship and add a cup of thoughtfulness. Cream together with a pinch of powdered tenderness, very lightly beaten, in a bowl of loyalty, with a cup of faith, one of hope and one of charity. Be sure to add a spoonful each of gaiety that sings and also ability to laugh at all the little things. Moisten with the sudden tears of heartfelt sympathy. Bake in a good-natured pan, and serve repeatedly.

— Author Unknown

Children

When daily chores all are ended,
And playtime for the day is dismissed,
And the little ones gather 'round me
To say goodnight prayers and be kissed,
Oh! the little white arms that encircle
My neck in tender embrace!
Oh! the smiles that are halos of Heaven
Shed sunshine of joy on my face!

When they're in their beds, I sit dreaming
Of my childhood, too lovely to last;
Of love that my heart well remembers
When it wakes to the rules of the past
'Fore I noticed the mean things around me,
Unaware of sorrow and sin—
Then, the glory of God was about me,
And the glory of gladness within.

O! my heart goes back to my children
And my thoughts and feeling flow
As I think of the path, steep and stony,
Where the feet of my dear ones must go;
Of the mountains of sin hanging o'er them,
Of the tempest of fate flowing wild;
Oh! there's nothing on earth half so holy
As the innocent heart of a child.

They are idols of hearts and of household!
They are angels of God, in disguise;
His sunlight still sleeps in their tresses,
His glory still gleams in their eyes.
Oh! those innocent dear ones from Heaven,
They make me so humble and mild;
And I know now how Jesus can liken
The kingdom of God to a child.

I ask not a life for my dear ones,
All radiant, as others have done;
But that life may have just enough shadow
To temper the glare of the sun.
I would pray God to guard them from evil—
Give them courage and strength to win
That their heads need never be bended
By regrets of "what might have been."

— Charles Dickens

No Man Is An Island

No man is an island;
No man stands alone.
Each man's joy is joy to me;
Each man's grief is my own.

We need one another,
So I will defend
Each man as my brother;
Each man as my friend.

I saw the people gather,
I heard the music start.
The song that they were singing
Is ringing in my heart.

No man is an island;
No man stands alone.
Each man's joy is joy to me;
Each man's grief my own.

We need one another,
So I will defend
Each man as my brother,
Each man as my friend.

— John Donne

The Little Things

It takes a little muscle, it takes a little grit,
A little true ambition with a little bit of wit.
It's not the biggest things that count,
and make the biggest show:
It's the little things that people do,
that make this old world go.

A little bit of smiling, and a little sunny chat,
A little bit of courage to a comrade slipping back.
It takes a kindly action, and it takes a work of cheer,
To fill a life with sunshine, and to drive away a tear.
Great things are not the biggest things
that make the biggest show;
It's the little things that people do,
that make this old world go.

— Author Unknown

CHAPTER SIX

Spirituality

SOLUTION

INTRODUCTION FOR PARENTS

A mother, wishing to encourage her son's progress at the piano, bought tickets to a Paderewski performance. When the evening arrived, they found their seats near the front of the concert hall and eyed the majestic Steinway piano waiting on the stage. Soon the mother found a friend to talk to, and the boy slipped away. At eight o'clock, the lights in the auditorium began to dim, the spotlights came on, and only then did they notice the boy—up on the piano bench, innocently picking out "Twinkle, Twinkle Little Star." His mother gasped, but before she could retrieve her son, the master appeared on the stage and quickly moved to the keyboard.

He whispered to the boy, "Don't quit. Keep playing." Leaning over, Paderewski reached down with his left hand and began filling in the bass part. Soon his right arm reached around the other side and improvised a delightful obligato. Together, the old master and the young novice held the crowd mesmerized.

In our lives, unpolished though we may be, it is God who surrounds us and whispers in our ear time and time again, "Don't quit. Keep playing." And as we do, he augments and supplements until a work of amazing beauty is created.

If you were to identify the foundation piece of your family, what would it be? May I share ours? The foundation for the Fellingham Family is spirituality. Our belief in God and our love for him help direct our lives and our decisions. This is not to say that either our lives or our decisions meet with God's approval. Nonetheless, we have a great desire that God be the rock upon which we are founded.

Being well aware that this is a sensitive subject and not wanting to offend, I approach the issue of spirituality carefully. Knowing that there are many ways to experience and express spirituality, I would like to simply share with you my interpretation of how spirituality works for our family in day-to-day living.

The four lessons in this chapter are Believe, Pray, Worship and Share. I would like to write about these parts of spirituality from experiences in my home. You may have different, highly effective ways of experiencing spirituality in your family. I would thoroughly enjoy hearing about them.

Believe

We believe that God exists and that he loves us. Because of these beliefs we look for God's hand in the beauties of the world. We give him gratitude and glory for all good things in our lives. Believing that God loves us gives our family a wonderful feeling of comfort and security—knowing that Someone is aware of us and cares about our lives. God sees our efforts to live correctly, and he knows the secret desires of our hearts. We also believe that when we fail, he will forgive and give us the strength to try again.

Because we believe that there is a "master plan" for this world and for each one of us, we feel there is a purpose for this life, and we believe that the things we do to improve our lives have meaning.

We believe that God has expectations for each of his children on the Earth, and he set forth rules and guidelines for us to follow. These rules were not made to be barriers and stumbling blocks, but rather to make our road smoother and to bring us joy through obedience. We have discovered as a family that when we are living in accordance with God's laws and commandments, we're happier. It is our belief that since God never forces his will on us, the principle of free agency is an important one. Our family has learned that we actually have more freedom when we make wise choices and obey God's laws.

Believing in God, seeking his help and guidance in our lives, and feeling his love for us has been an integral part of our family life.

Pray

Our family believes that God wants to help us and that he will help us according to his great wisdom and love. We ask for God's help when we speak with him in prayer. We've found that sometimes the way God helps us isn't exactly the way we wanted or expected his help. However, hindsight has shown us that his method of answering our prayers has always helped us learn and become better people.

Communicating with God through prayer has been a strength to us in times of need. In our immediate family we have experienced death and near death. Twice in hospital emergency rooms my husband and I have been told by doctors that they were sorry, but there was nothing modern medicine could do for our children. Additionally, I have struggled in relationships which have caused me heartache and deep disappointment. In my hours of emotional and spiritual need I have

---

Ways to Experience Spirituality

- **Believe:** God exists and he loves you.
- **Pray:** Reach out to God in faith that he will hear you and answer your prayers.
- **Worship:** Show God your love and devotion by putting him first.
- **Share:** Let others know about the good news of life that fills your heart with gratitude and hope.

turned to God in earnest prayer. I know that in those hours I was strengthened by God. He heard and answered my prayers.

Communicating with God? It sounds incredible. I believe, however, that prayer is a gift from a loving God. He cares about our well-being and happiness. Our family pray each morning before we go our separate ways, and then we kneel in prayer together at the end of each day. We also give thanks and ask a blessing upon our food. Then, as I mentioned, we pray during times of special need. I think that the formalities of what we say are not as important as the act of reaching out to God in faith that he will hear us.

Worship

Worship is defined as the act or feeling of adoration or homage; the paying of religious reverence as in prayer, praise, etc. The word adoration is defined as an emotion of profound admiration, utmost love and devotion. According to this definition, the things we worship in life are what we adore, admire, love and show devotion to. Does that describe our feelings about God?

That question helps us think about how we worship God. It causes us to reflect on the things to which we show devotion, and adore. I can't help but think about the days and weeks I've spent dreaming about and planning for homes we've built. I believe, however, that our hearts play a role in this matter. Where are our hearts? Do we treasure our possessions more than our relationships? Do we care more about accumulating money than we care about our family? Have we ever sought power or promotions at the expense of our integrity? I sincerely believe that every day, we show what it is we worship by the way we live our lives. We prove where our heart lies with every decision we make. The definition of worship helps us realize that if we truly worship God we'll try to live as he would have us live. In our family when we're faced with decisions, we try to remember to ask ourselves the question, "What would God have us do?" The answer is often obvious and simple.

Attending a weekly worship service as a family has also been a source of spiritual strength for us. As we gather weekly with those who believe as we do, we have the opportunity of learning more about God during the worship service, and also discerning who in our religious community may need our help. I believe that people truly worship God when they are obedient to his laws, when they're kind and unselfish, and when they love their fellowmen. Then, because of their good lives, others will want to know more about God.

Share

When you hear some really good news, what do you immediately want to do? You want to share it with someone. If it's really exciting, life-changing good news, you may want to shout it from the rooftops and tell the whole world. I believe that the strength and peace God can bring into your family's life is good news—life-changing good news.

It is very difficult to raise a good family. In the book *A Tale of Two Cities* author Charles Dickens wrote, "It was the best of times; it was the worst of times." Sometimes do you feel that way in your family? One moment you're discouraged and feel like a failure. The next moment something happens that fills your heart with gratitude and hope. Our families can be the source of our greatest concern and heartache, and also the source of our greatest joy and happiness.

I believe that we don't have to raise our families alone. We don't have to struggle through the years without help. God is there for all of us. God will help us if we turn to him, seeking his guiding power and influence in our lives.

LESSON TWENTY-ONE

Believe

Follow-up

(As a family discuss the assignment for the lesson Financial Well Being.)

1. What are some of the things we're doing to live within our budget?
2. What steps are we taking to save some of our money?

Concept

Believing in God means that we believe there is a God. We believe that he exists, even though we haven't seen him. We agree that there is abundant evidence of a "master plan" for this world and its people.

God loves us and he wants us to be happy. Believing this gives us faith that God cares about us individually and as a family. We trust that God will help us when we turn to him.

Families can experience peace and happiness when they use the truths found in scriptures and religious readings in their everyday lives. These truths can give life meaning, and they can give families direction. Scriptural truths can give people greater understanding of God's ways and a perspective of the "master plan." God has set forth rules and provided a path for us to follow. If we will live by his rules and walk down his path, we can have peace and enjoy greater happiness.

Discovering what God's plan is for us is one of life's great adventures. Living in harmony with that plan is one of life's greatest challenges.

Family Survey Review

Statement #21. We rely upon God.

- What does relying on God mean?
- How do we feel about the statement "God loves us and he wants us to be happy."

STORY

One evening a father and his four-year-old son Phillip had taken a ride in the country. They ran out of gas. After they had obtained some gas at a nearby farm house, the father and son were walking back to their car. The father was carrying the gas can. Phillip was playing as they walked, throwing rocks at the telephone poles, and picking flowers. Then all of a sudden, it got dark. Sometimes night comes all at once in the country. Philip came over, put his little hand in his father's and said, "Take my hand, Daddy. I might get lost."

There is a hand reaching to us from the heart of the universe. If we will lay our hand in the hand of God and walk with him, we will never, ever get lost.

Discussion

1. Do we believe there is a God who has a "master plan" for people on Earth?
2. How can we learn more about him and how his plan could improve our lives?
3. Should we pray together as a family? When?
4. What is spirituality? (*Example answer: Spirituality is allowing God to guide your life and living by his teachings and commandments.*)

Activity

As individuals and as a family, we should try to live the higher law of showing unconditional love to our fellowmen. If we do this, one of the blessings that will follow is a greater desire to serve others. We are God's hands on Earth.

The activity for this lesson is to choose a person or a family we can serve, and do an act of kindness for them. Let's decide what to do, then plan the activity. If we can serve others without them knowing it, all the better!

Assignment

Read the story below, and do one or more of the Solution Suggestions listed on the following page.

BELIEF

Sir Isaac Newton, the British scientist, once had a skillful mechanic make him a miniature replica of our solar system, with balls representing the planets, geared together by cogs and belts so as to move in harmony when cranked. Later, Newton was visited by a scientist friend who did not believe in God.

As Newton sat reading in his study with his mechanism on a large table near him, his friend stepped in. Scientist that he was, he recognized at a glance what was before him. Stepping up to it he slowly turned the crank, and with undisguised admiration watched the heavenly bodies all move in their relative speed in their orbits. Standing off a few feet he exclaimed, "My! What an exquisite thing this is! Who made it?" Without looking up from his book, Newton answered, "Nobody."

Quickly turning to Newton, the man said, "Evidently you did not understand the question. I asked who made this?" Looking up now, Newton solemnly assured him that nobody made it, but that the aggregation of matter so much admired had just happened to assume the form it was in. But the astonished scientist replied with some heat, "You must think I am a fool! Of course somebody made it! He is a genius, and I'd like to know who he is!"

Laying aside his book, Newton arose and laid a hand on his friend's shoulder. "This thing is but a puny imitation of a much grander system whose laws you know. I am not able to convince you that this mere toy is without a designer and maker; yet you profess to believe that the great original, from which the design is taken, has come into being without either designer or maker! Now tell me by what sort of reasoning do you reach such an incongruous conclusion?"

SPIRITUALITY

1. Pray together as a family.

2. Read scriptures or religious readings as a family.

3. Try meditation as a form of worship.

4. Each family member spend some time alone in nature thinking about God and the purpose of life.

5. Sing or listen to beautiful songs which tell of God and his goodness.

6. Learn about a specific spiritual subject.

7. Attend a church meeting as a family.

8. Do an anonymous act of kindness for another family.

9. Share a spiritual thought or feeling with a friend.

10. Make a list of as many of your blessings as you can. Talk about how much your family has to be grateful for.

LESSON TWENTY-TWO

Pray

Follow-up

(As a family, discuss the assignment for the lesson Believe.)

1. What was the activity we did from the Solution Suggestions list?
2. What did we learn from this activity?

Concept

Prayer is the act of communicating with God. It is an act of worship that usually involves talking and listening. The unspoken yearnings of our hearts that go up in supplication to God are also prayers. The formalities of what we say (in other words, how and what we say) are not as important as the act of reaching out to God in faith that he will hear us.

God wants to help us, and he will help us in accordance with his great wisdom and love, his knowledge of our true needs, and our worthiness and desire for his help.

There seem to be no limitations as to when, where, and what we should pray about.

Prayer is a powerful method of communicating our thoughts, needs and desires to One who can help us, strengthen us, and bless us in our efforts to become better people.

Four steps of prayer are suggested:

1. **Prepare.** As we prepare to speak to God, we should try to rid our mind of worldly thoughts and focus on him. For a moment we should contemplate God's greatness and goodness and think about what we'll say in our prayer.

2. **Express gratitude.** The second part of a prayer is to praise God and thank him for his blessings to us and to our family. We should thank God for specific things, expressing gratitude with all of our heart.

3. **Ask for help.** We should pray for specific ways God can help us, and seek forgiveness for our wrong-doings.

4. **Listen.** When we pray we seek God, and try to understand his will. How can we learn if we don't listen? We should keep our minds open and believing. During and after our prayers we should pause and listen, trying sincerely to receive insights—ideas that may help us. Divine impressions will come to us more readily when we're quiet and listen for them.

Family Survey Review

Statement #22. Our family prays together.

- Do you think God hears and answers prayers? How?
- Do we think praying as a family could help us? How?

STORY

Once there was an injured little orphan boy who was hurried to the hospital where it was determined that he needed an immediate operation. When he was wheeled into the operating room, he heard the doctors and nurses discussing his problem. He knew that it was very serious. The young boy spoke to a doctor as they were preparing to give him the anesthetic. "Doctor, before you begin to operate, will you please pray for me?"

The doctor, with seeming embarrassment, offered an excuse and said, "I can't pray for you." The boy asked the other doctor with the same result. Then the little boy said, "If you can't pray for me, will you please wait while I pray for myself?"

They removed the sheet and he knelt on the operating table. He bowed his head and said, "God, I am just an orphan boy, and I'm awful sick. Won't you please make me well? Bless these men who are going to operate that they'll do it right. If you will make me well, I'll try to grow up and be a good man. Thank you, God."

When the little boy was finished, he lay down. The doctors' and nurses' eyes were filled with tears. The child said, "I'm ready now."

The operation was performed. The boy was taken back to his room, and before long he was well on his way to recovery.

Sometime afterwards the experienced surgeon remarked, "I have operated on hundreds of people, men and women who thought they had faith to be healed. But never until I stood over that little boy have I felt the Spirit of God as I felt it then. That boy opened the windows of heaven and talked to his God as one would have talked to his friend, face to face. I want to say to you that I am a better man for having heard a little boy pray."

Discussion

1. Why did the little boy want to pray?
2. How did the surgeon feel about the boy's prayer?
3. How do we feel about prayer?

Activity

The activity for this lesson is to gather together and say a prayer as a family.

Assignment

The assignment is to lift your thoughts to God often and include him in your lives through prayer.

Also, read the Additional Solution for Success: The Healing Power of Prayer.

THE HEALING POWER OF PRAYER

This interesting discovery concerning prayer was reported by Dr. Larry Dorsey in the *Reader's Digest* in June, 1995:

It was during residency training at Parkland Memorial Hospital in Dallas, Texas, when I had my first patient with terminal cancer in both lungs. I advised him on what therapy was available and what little I thought it would do. Rightly enough, he opted for no treatment.

Yet whenever I stopped by his hospital bedside, he was surrounded by visitors from his church, singing and praying. *Good thing,* I thought, *because soon they'll be singing and praying at his funeral.*

A year later, when I was working elsewhere, a colleague at Parkland called to ask if I wanted to see my old patient. *See him?* I couldn't believe he was still alive. I studied his chest X rays and was stunned. The man's lungs were completely clear. There was no sign of cancer.

"His therapy has been remarkable," the radiologist said, looking over my shoulder.

Therapy? I thought. *There wasn't any—unless you consider prayer.*

I had long ago given up the faith of my childhood. Now, as an adult, I believed only in the power of modern medicine. Prayer seemed an arbitrary frill, and so I put the incident out of my mind.

The years passed, and I became chief of staff at a large urban hospital. I was aware that many of my patients used prayer, but I put little trust in it. Then, in the late 1980's, I began to come across studies, many conducted under stringent laboratory conditions, which showed that prayer brings about significant changes in a variety of physical conditions.

Perhaps the most convincing study, published in 1988, was by cardiologist Dr. Randolph Byrd. A computer assigned 393 patients at the coronary-care unit of the San Francisco General Hospital to one of two groups. Half were prayed for by prayer groups, and half were not remembered in prayer. No one knew to which group the patients belonged. The prayer groups were simply given the patients' first names, along with brief descriptions of their medical problems. They were asked to pray each day until the patient was discharged from the hospital, but were given no instructions on how to do it or what to say.

When the study was completed ten months later, the prayed-for patients benefitted in several significant areas:

- They were 5 times *less* likely than the unremembered group to require antibiotics.
- They were 2 times *less* likely to suffer congestive heart failure.
- They were *less* likely to suffer cardiac arrest.

If the medical technique being studied had been a new drug or surgical procedure instead of prayer, it would probably have been heralded as a breakthrough. Even hard-boiled skeptics like Dr. William Nolen, who had written a book questioning the validity of faith healing, acknowledged, "If this is a valid study, we doctors ought to be writing on our order sheets, "Pray three times a day." If it works, it works.

I *(Dr. Larry Dorsey)* have since given up practicing medicine to devote myself to researching and writing about prayer and how it affects our health. There are studies which suggest that prayer can have a beneficial effect on high blood pressure, wounds, headaches and anxiety. Here are some of the things I've found:

- **Prayer Can Take Many Forms.** In the studies I've seen, results occurred not only when people prayed for explicit outcomes but also when they prayed for nothing specific. Some studies, in fact, showed that a simple "Thy will be done" was more powerful than specific results held in the mind. In many experiments a simple attitude of prayerfulness, an all-pervading sense of holiness and a feeling of empathy, caring and compassion, seemed to set the stage for healing.

- **Love Increases the Power of Prayer.** The power of love is legendary. It is built into folklore, common sense and everyday experience. Throughout history, tender, loving care has uniformly been recognized as a valuable element in healing. In fact, a survey of 10,000 men with heart disease (published in *The Journal of American Medicine)* found close to a 50-percent reduction in frequency of angina in those who perceived their wives as supportive and loving.

- **Prayer Can Be Open-Ended.** Most people who pray are convinced that it can be used in a purposeful, goal-specific manner. But research shows that open-ended entreaties seem to work too. Invocations such as "Thy will be done," "Let it be," or "May the best thing happen" do not involve "using" prayer for specific outcomes, nor do they involve sending complicated messages.

Perhaps this is what some people mean when they advocate, "Let go and let God." Many recognize in their own prayers a spontaneous, uncontrollable quality that brings results.

• **Prayer Means You Are Not Alone.** A patient of mine was dying. The day before his death, I sat at his bedside with his wife and children. He knew he had little time left, and he chose his words carefully, speaking in a hoarse whisper. Although he was not a religious person, he revealed to us that recently he had begun to pray.

"What do you pray *for*?" I asked him.

"It isn't 'for' anything," he said thoughtfully. "It simply reminds me that I am not alone."

Prayer is like that. It is a reminder of our unbounded nature, of the part of us that is infinite in space and time. It is the universe's affirmation that we are not alone.

LESSON TWENTY-THREE

Worship

Follow-up

(As a family discuss the assignment for the lesson Pray.)

1. What do we each think about prayer?
2. When we're praying, and after praying, how do we feel?

Concept

Worship is defined as the act or feeling of adoration or homage; the paying of religious reverence as in prayer, praise, etc. The word *adoration* is defined as an emotion of profound admiration, utmost love and devotion.

According to this definition, the thing we worship in life is what we adore, admire, love and show devotion to. Does that describe our feelings about God?

How do people worship?

- **Prayer:** Communicating with God.
- **Meditation:** Connecting to (divine) energy within.
- **Formal Worship Services:** Attending meetings to learn about God.
- **Music:** Uplifting music to bring thoughts of divinity, gratitude, love.
- **Thoughts:** Directing thoughts toward God.

Think about the definition of worship as feelings of adoration, love and devotion. Does that describe how we feel about some of our possessions or activities in life? There are people who care so much about the accumulation of wealth or power that they neglect family relationships. Some people adore money, a large house or an expensive car. Is that what they worship? We may want to reflect on what it is that we worship. Spending time learning about God and building a strong, happy family is far more important than spending time accumulating more money than is necessary.

God is the same yesterday, today and forever. He loves us, and he wants us to love each other. God knows we can find true happiness by obeying his laws, and by loving and serving people unconditionally. Our actions show how sincerely we worship God.

Family Survey Review

Statement #23. We worship God as a family.

- How do we feel about worshiping together as a family?
- If worshiping together is something that will bring family unity and strength, should we consider attending a worship service as a family?

STORY

Once upon a time there were three men who were told they would have an interview in which they'd be asked to tell what they knew about God.

The first man entered the room and described to the interviewer in great detail all he had learned about God. He told about God's great wisdom and his omnipotent power. The man then described God's love and compassion. The interviewer listened with intense interest while the first man spoke. When the man was finished, the interviewer thanked him sincerely and excused him.

The second man entered the room. This gentleman was well-learned and regarded as an expert in religion. He began by explaining several different theories about God. This second man was well-prepared for the interview and presented a lengthy discourse on the Almighty. The interviewer listened attentively, then thanked the man for his time. The knowledgeable gentleman left the room.

The third man entered. As he looked into the face of the interviewer, he immediately fell to his knees and exclaimed, "My Lord, My God!"

The first two men knew many things about God. The third man knew God.

Discussion

1. When people worship, they can either give "lip service" (say the words and go through the motions without really meaning it) or they can worship God with their whole hearts and show by their actions what they believe. How do we worship?
2. What can we do to improve in this area of spirituality?

Activity

Our activity for this lesson is to attend a worship service as a family. Let's do this with open minds and hearts while trying to learn more about God and his plan for our lives. Let's talk about our experience afterward.

Assignment

Realizing that there are several ways to worship, choose one of the ways you haven't worshiped before and try it. For example, if you've never meditated, learn more about it, then try it.

Read the Additional Solutions for Success: Worship Through Music.

WORSHIP THROUGH MUSIC

Well-known composer Igor Stravinsky (1882-1971) proclaimed, "Music praises God. Music can praise him as well or better than the building of the church and all its decorations. Music is the church's greatest ornament." Indeed, music can be a powerful form of worship. It has been called the universal language, the language of God.

Many believe that God has inspired composers through the ages as they've created beautiful music. Stravinsky asserted, "Only God can create. I make music from music." He also admitted, "I regard my talents as God-given, and I have always prayed to him for strength to use them."

Composer Ludwig Van Beethoven (1770-1827) believed in God and his power to help him compose. He recorded his thoughts: "It was not a fortuitous meeting of chordal atoms that made the world; if order and beauty are reflected in the constitution of the universe, then there is a God. Therefore, I will submit myself to all inconsistency and will place all my confidence in your eternal goodness, O God!" Near the end of Beethoven's life he wrote: "I have no friend; I must live by myself. I know, however, that God is nearer to me than others. I go without fear to him; I have constantly recognized and understood him."

On March 27, 1808, Franz Joseph Haydn attended his last musical performance. The program featured his oratorio *The Creation*. He had finished the massive work at age sixty-six, saying it had been composed to inspire "the adoration and worship of the Creator" and to put the listener "in a frame of mind where he is most susceptible to the kindness and omnipotence of the Creator." Haydn recalled, "Never was I so devout as when I composed *The Creation*. I knelt down each day to pray to God to give me strength for my work." He told a friend, "When I was working on *The Creation*, I felt so impregnated with the Divine certainty that, before sitting down to the piano, I would quietly and confidently pray to God to grant me the talent that was needed to praise Him worthily." At the March, 1808, performance of his triumphant oratorio, the composer was determined that God would get all the glory for His work. As the music faded and the audience applauded enthusiastically, Haydn lifted his hands and said, "Not from me—from there, above, comes everything!"

Another great composer, Wolfgang Amadeus Mozart (1756-1791), also professed his belief in, and reliance upon, God. Mozart once wrote, "Let us put our trust in God and console ourselves with the thought that all is well, if it is in accordance with the will of the Almighty, as he knows best what is profitable and beneficial to our temporal happiness and our eternal salvation." With such a trusting attitude, his talent was unhindered by the doubts and uncertainty that have plagued many artists. Mozart's faith left him free to use the talent given him, and it flowed from him in a seemingly never-ending stream of inspiration.

Felix Mendelssohn's (1809-1847) composing career was based on a firm belief in divine inspiration: "I know perfectly well that no musician can make his thoughts or his talents different to what Heaven has made them."

Johann Sebastian Bach (1685-1750) also believed God and good music to be inseparable. Bach was a career church musician in Germany. He proclaimed, "Music's only purpose should be for the glory of God and the recreation of the human spirit."

George Frederick Handel (1685-1759), a contemporary of Bach, agreed that God will intervene and assist in the creation of music. In 1741, Handel was genuinely discouraged. His health was failing, audiences had deserted him, and he was deeply in debt. Seeing no hope for the future, his music, or his life, he was ready to retire in disgrace. It seems that God had other plans for Handel. Two challenges were almost simultaneously set before him to change his life and the map of the musical world. From a Dublin charity, Handel received a commission to compose a piece of music for a benefit concert. From Charles Jennings, a wealthy friend, he received a libretto based exclusively on Bible texts.

With that libretto in hand, Handel went into a feverish work mode. For three weeks, beginning on August 22, he confined himself to his small house on Brook Street in London. From early morning into the night, he rarely left his music paper, ink, and pens. A friend who visited at that time reported having seen Handel weeping with intense emotion. Later, as Handel related the compositional experience, he quoted St. Paul's words: "Whether I was in the body or out of my body when I wrote it, I know not."

At one point a servant came into Handel's room to deliver a tray of food. He reported having seen a wild expression in his employer's eyes; a weeping Handel refused the food and exclaimed, "I think I did see all Heaven before me, and the great God himself." George Frederick Handel had just completed what became the most-performed choral number in history, the "Hallelujah Chorus."

After six days of incredibly concentrated work, Handel had completed the first part of the *Messiah*. The second part took him nine days, and the third part took another six. In two more days, to complete the orchestration, the masterpiece called the *Messiah was* finished. In the unbelievably brief span of twenty-four days, Handel had filled two hundred sixty pages of manuscript. Musicologist Robert Myers stated that the music and its powerful message "has probably done more to convince thousands of mankind that there is a God about us than all the theological works ever written."

Yes, music is a powerful form of worship. In the words of J. S. Bach, "Where there is devotional music, God is always at hand with his gracious presence."

LESSON TWENTY-FOUR

Share

Follow-up

(As a family discuss the assignment for the lesson Worship.)

1. Have we attended a worship service together as a family? Should we plan to do that?
2. What have we learned about God since the lesson "Worship?"

Concept

Share is an action word which means to give a portion of what we have, or who we are, to others. As it relates to spirituality, it means to share things such as:

- love
- compassion
- friendship
- knowledge
- optimism
- time
- understanding
- courage

For example, when someone has a problem, we can give of ourselves by listening to him, and discussing possible solutions. If someone needs knowledge, a helping hand, or an understanding heart, we can share ours.

We can share our optimism (good attitude) by smiling and

being friendly. We can look for opportunities to share our time and compassion. We can forgive. We can love all people. There are countless ways to share.

There is a saying, "Giving (sharing) is its own reward—all that we send into the lives of others comes back into our own." It is a true principle that when we give, we also receive. Just as a successful farmer harvests plentifully after planting, we also will reap rewards—of joy—when we share our possessions with others, or when we share our talents and strengths with a happy heart.

Just as a person in darkness appreciates another's light, so we can share our spiritual light. How can we do this? To share a light, we must first have one. Believing, praying, learning, and worshiping are ways to increase our understanding of God, and to create that "light." Additionally, when we obey God's laws, show love to everyone, and tirelessly serve others, we will earn a light to share. At that point our life will be a bright beacon that can guide our fellowmen toward inner peace and true happiness.

Family Survey Review

Statement #24. We share our feelings about God in our family.

- How can sharing our feelings about God strengthen our family?
- What are some of the ways our family can share with others a portion of what we have or who we are?

STORY

Michelle was very unhappy. Everything in her life seemed wrong. She felt she was unattractive, that her personality was dull, and Michelle knew she had very few friends. Even her house was old and dingy.

One day Michelle made the decision to do something about her life. She went to Angela Swain, an attractive, popular, and talented woman who lived in a lovely cottage. Michelle poured out the story of her unhappy life. She told Angela all of the details—of her poverty, ugliness, disappointments and frustrations. Angela listened attentively. After a gentle word of sympathy she said, "You can change all that if you really have the will to do it."

"How? How?" cried Michelle. "I'll do anything, no matter how hard it is!"

Angela replied, "Will you? It's not difficult at all. It only takes time. You see, you must sow the seed for another kind of life, and wait with patience for it to grow. Here is the test to see if you truly have the will. Live for twenty-four hours as if God were right beside you seeing everything that you do. Then come back to me again, and we'll talk it over. Will you do that?"

Michelle had never thought of God as though he were a friend to whom one might speak. She replied, "Yes, Mrs. Swain, I will try anything."

It was late afternoon when Michelle went home. She knew she was expected to help get supper onto the table. She went to the drawer and took out a wrinkled tablecloth. When she spread it on the table, she noticed several soiled spots. Michelle then had her first thought of change.

"If God were going to eat with us, I wouldn't put on a soiled cloth," she said to herself.

She got a fresh cloth. With the same thought, she brought in a small bowl of flowers from the yard. Michelle put the butter on a fresh plate. She cut the bread with care. Instead of plain, boiled potatoes, she mashed and beat them lightly. She made her gravy smooth and rich.

"Company tonight?" asked her father, peering through his glasses as he came to the table.

"Just you, Daddy," smiled Michelle. If God were present, of course you'd smile at your family and show them your very best manner.

Her mother, worn and hot, exclaimed, "I don't know what's gotten into her to fix up so, just for us. I suppose she's expecting someone to drop in before we're done."

Michelle bit back a hasty retort. She kept still until she thought of the proper thing to say in the presence of the unseen Guest. "I don't know of anyone I would rather fix things up for than our own family," she said.

The family simply stared for a minute. That was not like Michelle. Then Father said, "That's right. It's too bad we all don't think of that more often." But Tom, her younger brother, snickered.

Michelle's anger flared. There was nothing more irritating than to be laughed at when trying to do your best. Michelle said to herself, "God is here," and said nothing aloud.

Tom was ashamed, but didn't say so. After dinner, Michelle's sister Karen said, "It's your turn to wash the dishes."

"All right," said Michelle. Usually there was a sharp argument over whose turn it was. Michelle got the water ready and began. After a while Karen blurted out, "It really was my turn, Michelle. I was selfish to let you wash. I'll take my turn tomorrow and the next day."

"It's all right, Karen. I really don't mind washing at all." To her astonishment, Michelle knew that this was true. When you don't mind washing, it stops being a hard job.

And the next day was the same. Michelle found that her thoughts of God helped her to be cheerful and to think of others. At work she met every customer with an eager interest to serve them well. Closing time came before she knew it.

Later that evening Michelle returned to Mrs. Angela Swain's home.

"I tried it, Mrs. Swain, just as well as I could. Imagining that God was beside me made everything different. It didn't change my circumstances. I still live in an old house, I am poor, and I—"

"Ah, my dear! But you only started the seed-sowing twenty-four hours ago. When you first put the seed in the ground, the garden doesn't look different, does it? That's the way with people. You say that your circumstances haven't changed, but you've started to improve them. You have the magic now. It is God. Just remember to keep your daily walk very close to him, and your life will change."

"I will do it," said Michelle. "I can do it, with him beside me."

Discussion

1. Do we sometimes feel discouraged with our lives, as Michelle did?
2. What were some of the changes Michelle made in her life?
3. What do you think about trying in your life to do what Michelle did?

Activity

The activity for this lesson is to gather as a family and share how we feel about God.

Also, let's discuss our feelings about our family. Last, let's talk about what we have learned from the Solutions for Families program.

Assignment

Read the Additional Solution for Success: Sharing Strengthens Families.

Since this is the last assignment in *Solutions for Families,* you may wish to share the program with another family. If you've benefitted from the lessons and gained strength from the concepts, share your insights and experiences with others. Again, every time you share, every time you give of yourselves, you'll receive sweet rewards far better than money can buy.

May God's richest blessings be yours as you bless the lives of others.

SHARING STRENGTHENS FAMILIES

By definition, family is more than one. Family is never "I," it is always "we." As a family member, we shouldn't simply focus on our desires alone. To be successful we need to think beyond ourselves and give to others. Creating a good family requires service and sacrifice, but joy always comes from loving and serving others. No matter what our circumstances, we can each give of ourselves and share something, every day of our lives. We can share a smile, a warm greeting, a kind word, a listening ear. Albert Schweitzer, a well-known humanitarian, once wrote:

> "Open your eyes and look for some man, or some work for the sake of men, which needs a little time, a little friendship, a little sympathy, a little sociability, a little human toil. It is needed in every nook and corner. Therefore search and see if there is not some place where you may invest your humanity."

The following story about a sister and brother helps us understand that the most important way we can give is to share a part of ourselves.

> The violent grinding of brakes suddenly applied and the harsh creaking of skidding wheels gradually died away as the big car came to a stop. Eddie quickly picked himself up from the dusty pavement where he had been thrown and looked wildly around.
>
> Linda! Where was the little sister he had been holding by the hand when they started to cross the street? The next moment he saw her under the big car that had run them down. With one bound, the boy was under the car, trying to lift the child.
>
> "You'd better not try, son," said a man gently. "Someone has gone for help."
>
> "She's not...dead, is she?" Eddie begged.
>
> The man stooped and felt the limp little pulse. "No, my boy," he said slowly.
>
> A policeman came, dispersed the collecting crowd, and carried the unconscious girl into a nearby store. Eddie's

folded coat made a pillow for her head until the ambulance arrived. He was permitted to ride in the ambulance with her to the hospital. Something about the sturdy, shabbily dressed boy, only ten years old, and his devotion to his little sister, touched the hearts of the hospital attendants.

"We must operate at once," said the surgeon after a brief preliminary examination. "She has been injured internally and has lost a great deal of blood." He turned to Eddie who stood close by. "Where do you live?"

Eddie told him that their father was dead and that their mother did day work. He didn't know where.

"We can't wait to find her," said the surgeon, "because by that time it might be too late."

Eddie waited in the sitting area while the surgeons worked on Linda. After what seemed like an eternity, a nurse emerged from the operating room.

"Eddie," she said kindly, "your sister is doing very badly and the doctor wants to give her a transfusion. Do you know what that is?" Eddie shook his head. "Linda has lost so much blood she cannot live unless someone gives her his. Will you do it for her?"

Eddie's face grew paler, and he gripped the knobs of the chair hard. For a moment he hesitated; then gulping back his tears, he nodded and stood up.

"That's a good boy," said the nurse.

She patted his head, and led the way to the elevator which took them to the operating room. No one spoke to Eddie except the nurse, who directed him in a low voice how to prepare for the ordeal. The boy bit his quivering lip and obeyed.

"Are you ready?" asked a man dressed in white, turning from the table over which he had been working. For the first time Eddie noticed Linda, lying so still on the table. His little sister....and he was going to make her well!

Eddie stepped forward quickly.

Two hours later the surgeon looked up with a smile into the faces of the young interns and nurses who were engrossed in watching the great man work.

"Fine," he said. "I think she will live."

After the transfusion Eddie had been told to lie quietly on a cot in the corner of the room. In the concern for the delicate operation Eddie had been forgotten.

"It was wonderful, Doctor!" exclaimed one of the young interns. "A miracle!" Nothing, he felt in his enthusiastic recognition of the marvels of surgery, could be greater than the miracles of science.

"I am well satisfied," said the surgeon with pride.

There was a tug at his sleeve, but he didn't notice. In a little while there was another tug, and the great surgeon glanced down to see a pale-faced boy looking steadily up into his face.

"Doctor," said Eddie timidly, "when do I die?"

The interns laughed and the great surgeon smiled. "Why, what do you mean, my boy?" he asked kindly.

"I thought—when they took somebody's blood—he died," muttered Eddie.

The smiles faded from the lips of the doctors and nurses, and the young intern who had thought there was nothing greater than the miracles of science, caught his breath suddenly. This young boy had climbed to the very height of nobility and sacrifice, and had showed them a glimpse of the greatest miracle of all—unconditional love.

There was a long pause before the surgeon answered softly, "You will both get well, Eddie—you and your little sister."

All who witnessed Eddie's act of selfless giving would never forget him.

SPIRITUALITY

Love Your Fellowman

A boat was sinking somewhere off the Pacific Northwest Coast during a violent storm. A crowd had gathered to watch the battered vessel being pounded to pieces on the rocks off shore. Some sturdy men launched a lifeboat and pulled frantically at the oars to reach the ship in time to rescue the seamen who clung to their fast-disintegrating vessel.

As the small life boat came struggling back to shore, someone cried out, "Did you save them?"

"All but one," came the answer through the storm. "There was one we couldn't reach."

Then a young man stepped forth from the group and called, "Who will come with me to get the other man?"

His gray-haired mother cried out, "Oh Jim, please don't go! Please don't risk your life—you are all that I have left."

Onlookers knew that this boy's father had been drowned at sea, and years ago his brother, Bill, had sailed away and had never been heard from since.

But the boy replied, "Mother, someone has to go." A few others joined him and together they launched their boat and pulled from the wreck, while those on shore anxiously waited.

Finally, the boat was seen pulling away from the wreck and heading again for shore. The crowd watched as the small frail craft was beaten by the wave. At every plunge of the boat it looked as if it would be crushed like an eggshell. There was silence on the shore as the watchers prayed. For an hour the desperate struggle continued until the lifeboat was near enough to hail. Someone shouted, "Did you get the other man?"

Then in a high, clear, triumphant shout over the roar of the surf came the young man's voice saying, "Yes, and tell mother that the man we rescued is Bill!"

— Author Unknown

For the Sake of Giving

John Chapman, a nurseryman in Pennsylvania, loved all the beautiful things in the world. He especially loved his great apple orchards when they were in bloom in the spring and when they were loaded with luscious fruit in the fall. He wished everyone could have an apple orchard. He was generous with the young trees and apple seeds. To the many families moving west, to make new homes, who came to buy young trees, he gave apples for their journeys and seeds, as well as saplings for the orchards they would start in distant prairie lands.

When discouraging letters came back to him stating that the saplings and seeds did not grow, he felt that it was because the pioneers did not know how to care for their young orchards. This worried him. He thought of the blessings apple orchards would be out in the new country.

He decided he must go himself to the new frontier. It was "as if he heard a call to go and plant orchards in the new land, to give apple trees to the pioneers." So John Chapman dedicated the rest of his life to giving.

He collected all the apple seeds he could buy or beg and made arrangements so that he could send for more. Then he went out into the wilderness, vowing that with God's help he would give the flowers and the fruit of a thousand orchards to the discouraged homesteaders.

He endured many hardships and dangers as he traveled. He planted orchards next to isolated cabins and churches, and in many communities. As the orchards grew they helped to bring love and hope and joy where there had been only bitterness and despair.

As the years went by, the trees in orchard after orchard took root and bore blossoms and fruit. The settlers named him Johnny Appleseed. He had the satisfaction of knowing that he had given a priceless gift to humanity. He said that the only reward he hoped for was that there would be orchards to plant and nurture in heaven. Truly Johnny Appleseed gave of himself for the sake of giving.

— Eleanor Atkinson

Recipe for Success

To laugh often and much; to win the respect of intelligent people and the affection of children; to earn the appreciation of honest critics and endure the betrayal of false friends; to appreciate beauty; to find the best in others; to leave the world a bit better, whether by a healthy child, a garden patch, or a redeemed social condition; to know even one life has breathed easier because you lived—this is to have succeeded.

— Ralph Waldo Emerson

The Bridge Builder

An old man traveling a long highway,
Came at the evening cold and gray,
To a chasm vast and deep and wide,
The old man crossed in the twilight dim,
The sullen stream held no fears for him;
But he turned when safe on the other side,
And built a bridge to span the tide.

"Old man," cried a fellow pilgrim near,
"You're wasting your time in building here.
"Your journey will end with the closing day;
"You never again will pass this way.
"You have crossed the chasm deep and wide,
"Why build you this bridge at even-tide?"

The builder lifted his old gray head;
"Good friend, in the path I have come," he said.
"There followeth after me today
"A youth whose feet must pass this way,
"This stream which has been as naught to me,
"To that fair-haired youth may a pitfall be;
"He, too, must cross in the twilight dim—
"Good friend, I am building this bridge for him."

— Will Allen Dromgoole

A Prayer

Where there is hatred, let me sow love. Where there is injury, pardon. Where there is doubt, faith. Where there is despair, hope. Where there is darkness, light. Where there is sadness, joy. O divine Master, grant that I may not so much seek to be consoled as to console; to be understood, as to understand; to be loved, as to love; for it is in giving that we receive; it is in pardoning that we are pardoned, and it is in dying that we are born to Eternal Life.

— Francis of Assisi

A Prayer for Parents

O! Give me patience when little hands,
Tug at me with ceaseless small demands.
O! Give me gentle words and smiling eyes,
And keep my lips from hasty sharp replies.
Let me not in weariness, confusion or noise,
Obscure my vision from life's few fleeting joys.
Then when in years to come, my home is still,
No bitter memories, its rooms may fill.

— Author Unknown

I Knelt to Pray

I knelt to pray as day began
And prayed, "O God, bless every man.
Lift from each weary heart some pain
And let the sick be well again."

And then I rose to meet the day
And thoughtlessly went on my way:
I didn't try to dry a tear
Or take the time a grief to hear.
I took no steps to ease the load
Of hard-pressed travelers on the road;

I didn't even go to see
The sick friend who lives next door to me.

But then again when the day was done
I prayed, "O God, bless everyone."
But as I prayed a voice rang clear
Instructing me to think and hear.

"Consult your own heart ere you pray;
What good have you performed today?
God's choicest blessings are bestowed
On those who help him bear the load."

And then I hid my face and cried,
"Forgive me, Lord, for I have lied.
Let me live another day
And I will live it as I pray."

— Sterling W. Sill

High Resolve

I'll hold my candle high, and
Then perhaps I'll see the hearts of men
Above the sordidness of life,
Beyond misunderstandings, strife.
Though many deeds that others do
Seem foolish, rash and sinful, too,
Just who am I to criticize
What I perceive with my dull eyes?
I'll hold my candle high, and then
Perhaps I'll see the hearts of men.

— Author Unknown

The Sin of Omission

It isn't the thing you do;
It's the thing you leave undone,
Which gives you a bit of heartache
At the setting of the sun.

The tender word forgotten,
The letter you did not write,
The flower you might have sent,
Are your haunting ghosts tonight.

The stone you might have lifted
Out of a brother's way,
The bit of heartsome counsel
You were hurried too much to say.

The loving touch of the hand,
The gentle and winsome tone,
That you had no time or thought for
With troubles enough of your own.

The little acts of kindness,
So easily out of mind;
Those chances to be helpful
Which everyone may find—

No, it's not the thing you do,
It's the thing you leave undone,
Which gives you the bit of heartache
At the setting of the sun.

— Margaret E. Sanster

EVALUATION

Congratulations! You have made a remarkable effort as you've participated in *Solutions for Families*. Be confident in the knowledge that as you strengthen your family, our world becomes a better place. Former British Prime Minister Margaret Thatcher said it well: "Perhaps the world, at long last, is recognizing that strong families play a vital role in the stability of nations, and indeed the world."

If you have completed the book, your family has had lessons on kindness, commitment, communication, choices, well-being and spirituality. You have participated in many activities and discussions relating to these subjects.

Please return now to the Family Survey at the beginning of the book. To complete the *Solutions for Families* program, all family members should re-take the survey. Answer all of the questions again. Make a new graph and talk about the progress you've made toward your goals.

As a family, discuss what you have learned as you've participated in *Solutions for Families*. Continue using the resources in the book: the lessons; additional solutions for success; the many stories, poems and activities.

If you have any stories, information or "solutions for success" which can strengthen other families, I invite and encourage you to share them. To send your material or receive more information about Families Worldwide programs, contact:

FAMILIES NOW! Inc.
P.O. Box 37
Austin, Texas 78767-0037

In conclusion, I would again like to thank all who contributed to *Solutions for Families*. Additionally, I would like to thank you, the reader and participant. Without your interest and desire to strengthen your family, my efforts to share would be futile. For your interest, all author profits from the sale of this book go towards helping needy families—worldwide—who seek solutions.

May God's richest blessings be yours as you continue your efforts to strengthen your family, and as you reach out to strengthen others.

REFERENCES

Work in the Home: Building Enduring Relationships, Bahr, Dr. Kathleen Slaugh: 1998, Brigham Young University

Bringing Out the Winner, John Croyle: 1996, Cumberland House Publishing, Inc.

Catholic Questions, Catholic Answers, Fr. Kenneth Ryan: 1991, Servant Publications.

Celebrating Family Strengths Facilitator Manual: Southwest Prevention Center, College of Continuing Education, University of Oklahoma.

Chicken Soup For The Soul, Jack Canfield and Mark Victor Hansen: 1993, Health Communications, Inc.

Chicken Soup For The Soul, A Fourth Course, Jack Canfield and Mark Victor Hansen: 1997, Health Communications, Inc.

Chicken Soup For The Soul, A Third Serving, Jack Canfield and Mark Victor Hansen: 1996, Health Communications, Inc.

Especially For Mormons, Stan and Sharon Miller: 1973, Kellirae Arts

Families In Focus Home Learning Guide, Bernie Boswell: 1990, A Division of Chequemate International, Inc.

For Love And Money, Bernard E. Poduska: 1993, Brooks/Cole Publishing Co.

How To Make Your Child A Winner, Victor B. Cline: 1980, Walker and Company

Mother Teresa: The Authorised Biography, Navin Chawla, 1992, Element Books, Inc.

Prayer, N. Eldon Tanner: 1977, Deseret Book Company

Reader's Digest, "The Healing Power of Prayer," Larry Dorsey: 1995, June issue, Reader's Digest Association, Inc.

Roots And Wings, Helen Ream Bateman: 1983, Deseret Book Company

Secrets Of Strong Families, Nick Stinnet and John DeFrain: 1989, John Hancock Publishing

Speaker's Sourcebook II, Glenn Van Ekeren: 1994, Prentice-Hall, Inc.

Spiritual Moments With The Great Composers, Patrick Kavanaugh: 1995, Zondervan Publishing House

Strong Family, Charles R. Swindall: 1991, Zondervan Publishing House

The Family Virtues Guide, Linda Kavelin Popov: 1997, Penguin Books USA Inc.

World Religions, Chris Richards: 1997, Element Books Inc.

ABOUT THE AUTHOR

Paula Noble Fellingham is on the international forefront of the movement to strengthen families. She speaks at conferences and seminars worldwide, and actively assists numerous pro-family organizations. Paula has been the Executive Director of Families Worldwide, Inc., Vice President of eFamily.com, and President of Families Now, Inc. She founded the non-profit organization Solutions For Families, Inc., which currently endeavors to strengthen families in nations throughout the world.

Mrs. Fellingham was an educator for sixteen years. Additionally, she broadcasted the popular family segment on the coast-to-coast radio program "Celebrate," and now hosts her own daily radio show, *Solutions For Families*. Paula produced the highly successful parenting video *Creating A Successful Family*, and the parenting manual "Turn on the Light of Love and Learning in Your Home."

The Fellingham family performed as a family musical group across the nation and internationally for twelve summers. Paula has been honored as American Mothers Washington State Young Mother of the Year. She is the wife of Dr. Gilbert Fellingham and the mother of seven children.

Books by Paula Fellingham:

Solutions For Families
24 Lessons To Strengthen Relationships At Home

Believe...Achieve!
From Wishful Thinking To Dynamic Doing
co-authored with Lauralee Christiansen

How To Live So People Love You
Simple Ways to Become Loved and Admired

The Book of Values
76 Character-Strengthening Lessons
For Children

The Twelve Absolute Laws
For Practically Perfect Relationships

Raise Great Kids!
125 Ways To Be A Great Parent

Once Upon A Family
A Story of How To Raise Children Right

F A M I L Y   S U R V E Y

Name_____

Step 1: Choose the number below that you think is the most correct for each statement.

On the left, respond to the statement the way you think your family is now (actual).

On the right, respond the way you would like your family to be (ideal).

Almost Never	**Sometimes**	**Almost Always**
1	**3**	**5**

Actual   Ideal

_____   1. Our family thinks kind thoughts about one another.   _____

_____   2. In our family we express love for each other.   _____

_____   3. We use a kind tone of voice when we speak.   _____

_____   4. We treat one another the way we like to be treated.   _____

_____   5. We enjoy doing things together as a family.   _____

_____   6. We set family goals together.   _____

_____   7. Our family helps one another without being asked.   _____

_____   8. We have family traditions.   _____

_____   9. We try to understand one another's feelings.   _____

_____   10. We speak kindly to one another and try not to criticize.   _____

_____   11. We listen to each other.   _____

_____   12. In our family we can say what we feel.   _____

_____   13. We take responsibility for our own mistakes.   _____

_____   14. We all help make the rules in our family.   _____

_____   15. We try to prevent problems before they occur.   _____

_____   16. We can talk about things without arguing.   _____

_____   17. Our family has good health habits.
           (We eat healthfully, exercise regularly.)   _____

_____   18. We enjoy learning in our family.   _____

_____   19. Our family enjoys being with other people.   _____

_____   20. Our family makes wise financial decisions.   _____

_____   21. We rely upon God.   _____

_____   22. Our family prays together.   _____

_____   23. We worship God as a family.   _____

_____   24. We share our feelings about God in our family.   _____

_____ **Total**   **Total** _____

FAMILY SURVEY

Name_____

Step 1: Choose the number below that you think is the most correct for each statement.

On the left, respond to the statement the way you think your family is now (actual).

On the right, respond the way you would like your family to be (ideal).

Almost Never	**Sometimes**	**Almost Always**
1	**3**	**5**

Actual   Ideal

_____   1. Our family thinks kind thoughts about one another.   _____

_____   2. In our family we express love for each other.   _____

_____   3. We use a kind tone of voice when we speak.   _____

_____   4. We treat one another the way we like to be treated.   _____

_____   5. We enjoy doing things together as a family.   _____

_____   6. We set family goals together.   _____

_____   7. Our family helps one another without being asked.   _____

_____   8. We have family traditions.   _____

_____   9. We try to understand one another's feelings.   _____

_____   10. We speak kindly to one another and try not to criticize.   _____

_____   11. We listen to each other.   _____

_____   12. In our family we can say what we feel.   _____

_____   13. We take responsibility for our own mistakes.   _____

_____   14. We all help make the rules in our family.   _____

_____   15. We try to prevent problems before they occur.   _____

_____   16. We can talk about things without arguing.   _____

_____   17. Our family has good health habits.
                (We eat healthfully, exercise regularly.)   _____

_____   18. We enjoy learning in our family.   _____

_____   19. Our family enjoys being with other people.   _____

_____   20. Our family makes wise financial decisions.   _____

_____   21. We rely upon God.   _____

_____   22. Our family prays together.   _____

_____   23. We worship God as a family.   _____

_____   24. We share our feelings about God in our family.   _____

_____ **Total**   **Total** _____

F A M I L Y   S U R V E Y

Name_____

Step 1: Choose the number below that you think is the most correct for each statement.

On the left, respond to the statement the way you think your family is now (actual).

On the right, respond the way you would like your family to be (ideal).

Almost Never	**Sometimes**	**Almost Always**
1	**3**	**5**

Actual   Ideal
_____   1. Our family thinks kind thoughts about one another.   _____
_____   2. In our family we express love for each other.   _____
_____   3. We use a kind tone of voice when we speak.   _____
_____   4. We treat one another the way we like to be treated.   _____
_____   5. We enjoy doing things together as a family.   _____
_____   6. We set family goals together.   _____
_____   7. Our family helps one another without being asked.   _____
_____   8. We have family traditions.   _____
_____   9. We try to understand one another's feelings.   _____
_____   10. We speak kindly to one another and try not to criticize.   _____
_____   11. We listen to each other.   _____
_____   12. In our family we can say what we feel.   _____
_____   13. We take responsibility for our own mistakes.   _____
_____   14. We all help make the rules in our family.   _____
_____   15. We try to prevent problems before they occur.   _____
_____   16. We can talk about things without arguing.   _____
_____   17. Our family has good health habits.
               (We eat healthfully, exercise regularly.)   _____
_____   18. We enjoy learning in our family.   _____
_____   19. Our family enjoys being with other people.   _____
_____   20. Our family makes wise financial decisions.   _____
_____   21. We rely upon God.   _____
_____   22. Our family prays together.   _____
_____   23. We worship God as a family.   _____
_____   24. We share our feelings about God in our family.   _____

_____ **Total**   **Total** _____

FAMILY SURVEY

Name_____

Step 1: Choose the number below that you think is the most correct for each statement.

On the left, respond to the statement the way you think your family is now (actual).

On the right, respond the way you would like your family to be (ideal).

Almost Never	Sometimes	Almost Always
1	3	5

Actual   Ideal

____   1. Our family thinks kind thoughts about one another. ____

____   2. In our family we express love for each other. ____

____   3. We use a kind tone of voice when we speak. ____

____   4. We treat one another the way we like to be treated. ____

____   5. We enjoy doing things together as a family. ____

____   6. We set family goals together. ____

____   7. Our family helps one another without being asked. ____

____   8. We have family traditions. ____

____   9. We try to understand one another's feelings. ____

____ 10. We speak kindly to one another and try not to criticize. ____

____ 11. We listen to each other. ____

____ 12. In our family we can say what we feel. ____

____ 13. We take responsibility for our own mistakes. ____

____ 14. We all help make the rules in our family. ____

____ 15. We try to prevent problems before they occur. ____

____ 16. We can talk about things without arguing. ____

____ 17. Our family has good health habits.
        (We eat healthfully, exercise regularly.) ____

____ 18. We enjoy learning in our family. ____

____ 19. Our family enjoys being with other people. ____

____ 20. Our family makes wise financial decisions. ____

____ 21. We rely upon God. ____

____ 22. Our family prays together. ____

____ 23. We worship God as a family. ____

____ 24. We share our feelings about God in our family. ____

____ **Total**   **Total** ____

F A M I L Y   S U R V E Y

Name_____

Step 1: Choose the number below that you think is the most correct for each statement.

On the left, respond to the statement the way you think your family is now (actual).

On the right, respond the way you would like your family to be (ideal).

Almost Never	**Sometimes**	**Almost Always**
1	**3**	**5**

Actual   Ideal

_____   1. Our family thinks kind thoughts about one another.   _____

_____   2. In our family we express love for each other.   _____

_____   3. We use a kind tone of voice when we speak.   _____

_____   4. We treat one another the way we like to be treated.   _____

_____   5. We enjoy doing things together as a family.   _____

_____   6. We set family goals together.   _____

_____   7. Our family helps one another without being asked.   _____

_____   8. We have family traditions.   _____

_____   9. We try to understand one another's feelings.   _____

_____   10. We speak kindly to one another and try not to criticize.   _____

_____   11. We listen to each other.   _____

_____   12. In our family we can say what we feel.   _____

_____   13. We take responsibility for our own mistakes.   _____

_____   14. We all help make the rules in our family.   _____

_____   15. We try to prevent problems before they occur.   _____

_____   16. We can talk about things without arguing.   _____

_____   17. Our family has good health habits.
      (We eat healthfully, exercise regularly.)   _____

_____   18. We enjoy learning in our family.   _____

_____   19. Our family enjoys being with other people.   _____

_____   20. Our family makes wise financial decisions.   _____

_____   21. We rely upon God.   _____

_____   22. Our family prays together.   _____

_____   23. We worship God as a family.   _____

_____   24. We share our feelings about God in our family.   _____

_____ **Total**   **Total** _____

FAMILY SURVEY

Name_____

Step 1: Choose the number below that you think is the most correct for each statement.

On the left, respond to the statement the way you think your family is now (actual).

On the right, respond the way you would like your family to be (ideal).

Almost Never	**Sometimes**	**Almost Always**
1	**3**	**5**

Actual   Ideal

_____   1. Our family thinks kind thoughts about one another.   _____

_____   2. In our family we express love for each other.   _____

_____   3. We use a kind tone of voice when we speak.   _____

_____   4. We treat one another the way we like to be treated.   _____

_____   5. We enjoy doing things together as a family.   _____

_____   6. We set family goals together.   _____

_____   7. Our family helps one another without being asked.   _____

_____   8. We have family traditions.   _____

_____   9. We try to understand one another's feelings.   _____

_____   10. We speak kindly to one another and try not to criticize.   _____

_____   11. We listen to each other.   _____

_____   12. In our family we can say what we feel.   _____

_____   13. We take responsibility for our own mistakes.   _____

_____   14. We all help make the rules in our family.   _____

_____   15. We try to prevent problems before they occur.   _____

_____   16. We can talk about things without arguing.   _____

_____   17. Our family has good health habits.
            (We eat healthfully, exercise regularly.)   _____

_____   18. We enjoy learning in our family.   _____

_____   19. Our family enjoys being with other people.   _____

_____   20. Our family makes wise financial decisions.   _____

_____   21. We rely upon God.   _____

_____   22. Our family prays together.   _____

_____   23. We worship God as a family.   _____

_____   24. We share our feelings about God in our family.   _____

_____ **Total**   **Total** _____